Mysterious Grace

ALANA RUDKOVSKY

ISBN-13: 978-0-692-51925-7

Library of Congress Control Number: 2016918697
Lighthouse, Reston, VIRGINIA

DEDICATION

For Willow

CONTENTS

INTRODUCTION

Not thinking is the new way of thinking. We will become the receivers of divine thoughts and ideas. Even when you don't think, thoughts will still occur and action will still happen. The first major barrier is having faith in this. If you believe this, then the voice of the little self will begin to diminish and existence will be allowed to be as it is. To understand deep spiritual truth you don't need an advanced degree. In fact, this is often a hindrance to true understanding. There is a world which we experience through the senses, such as sight and sound, and there is another world which is quite apart from this rationality.

For some the spiritual path can only be embarked upon through suffering. For others it may happen within both the happiness and sadness of this world. Regardless, the type of spirituality we are referring to here involves no words or concepts of self. You are as you are and God is as He is. This is the stark, experiential being of enlightenment.

This book is about the voice of the little self in your head, or as it's commonly referred to, the ego. You might be shocked to find out it's not you. It is someone entirely different from the real you and from the peace and joy that the real you wants. All spirituality and religion points to the same truth: there is a false identity created by the mind which forces you into illusion and conflict, and when you let go of this identity, you become free. You have been living with this illusion for thousands of years. It's nothing personal and it's present in all of us, to varying degrees. You need to look at this identity closer and to decide if you still want to listen to it. Sometimes this sense of self is nice and pleasant, at other times it is awful, but at all times it is an illusion that lives in thought and you must watch it to get rid of it. It is common, not personal, which explains why so many of us suffer from similar distressing thoughts. Once you are able to transcend this, the true "I" will emerge in its perfect, non-dualistic form.

This is liberation. This is why we're all here. To be spiritual or religious doesn't mean that there is a story you believe in. It simply means that you want to know who you really are and why you're here, and most importantly, you want to stop wasting your precious energy. You want to know if all this suffering is necessary and how it came to be. You want to watch closely the thoughts you are feeding your mind. In this way, true spirituality is about self-purification. It is not a belief system, but a *being* system. And why is it so important to experience being? Because that is essentially what you are; pure life, experiencing itself in form.

Nothing new can be created, and you were created in the image and likeness of the Father. Your highest nature is already alive within you and just like everything else in the universe, it can never be destroyed. Meanwhile, your inner, self-created enemy of delusion tries to build a bigger army, which implies a false focus on the outside world and material power. But ultimately, we find that there is no material power and that our perceived materiality is actually created by things which we cannot readily identify with the senses.

Consciousness is the only truth and it encompasses everything. Both the good and the bad that you see around you is a play of consciousness temporarily hidden in form because the visible depends on and is molded by the invisible. When we shed this form, our true essence will be able to shine though. This is the only fight, and it is within. This is the central message of spirituality because it determines everything about your life here on Earth.

Why don't more people wish to pursue the spiritual path? Why do they wish to remain victims? Walk into any bookstore and you'll see that 80% of the books are fiction, be it romance or fantasy, basically anything that the ego makes up and finds entertaining, and the self-help/transformative section makes up less than 10%. People proudly look for their fiction books and then try to hide when anyone sees them browsing the self-help isle. We complain that we are helpless victims in a cruel world, but we not only fail to do anything about it, we continually propagate the delusion by giving it all of our attention.

Whatever you focus on determines all aspects of your life. You were placed in a highly sophisticated machine, which is your body, and you weren't told how to operate it properly. Now, you either choose to remain spiritually weak, subject to the laws of your own deprivation, or you ascend to wonderful heights of bliss and ease. You become Christ-like, which is what Jesus wanted for everyone. We are all children of God because in truth we are all consciousness, or part of God. Children do not worry about tomorrow, because they know they are taken care of. They live blissfully and they are provided for. They are here to experience joy.

However, this lifetime is here for you to learn to let go so that we can collectively take our next evolutionary steps and awaken. The path to liberation may not be easy at first, which is why this book is here to help. Carry it around with you throughout the day and apply it whenever possible, especially if you find yourself becoming stressed or unhappy. You let go of delusion by transcending it, and the first step is to watch your inner state diligently.

By "watch" we are referring to a state of alert awareness. When we watch we step away from the incessant and automatic activities of the personality. We become aware of *being* right where we are. When you sit down to meditate, the chief aim is to watch your thoughts as if they belonged to someone else – detached observation. This doesn't need to be done on a meditation mat in silence, and works just as well if you can keep this state of alert watchfulness throughout your day. It is similar to watching a movie, only you are watching your own life. We were always meant to watch it and to experience it with ease, and when we struggle, we get in the way of the inherent perfection. This is what is meant by detached awareness.

At the end of this, you will hopefully arrive at the truth which you have always known but have been unable to express: you are so much more than what can be seen on Earth. You will transform yourself, and thereafter you will transform the world in the only way that it can be transformed – through one person at a time.

We live in the heaviest land, suppressed by desires, engaging in constant mental activity, and unknowingly looking for trouble. To find love in the midst of all this is our only true purpose, and it will take us to higher and higher states of being. This is the first step on our journey toward the release of matter consciousness. We will explore our collective brain and where we're going and how we're interacting with one another in this incredible space. We will look at what we can accomplish, what is possible, probable even, given our natural propensity toward growth and exploration. We will set aside our unconscious propensity toward plainness, and we will step inside the mysterious.

CHAPTER 1

Observing Ourselves

Life is in a constant pendulum swing from day to night and birth to death. When we are born we are closest to the source, but then the pendulum swings away and if we aren't awake or conscious enough, we will unknowingly swing ourselves away from God. As adults, most of us are extremely removed from the true source of who we are and fully absorbed in who we aren't. We fill our days with commutes, structure, jobs, money, and worries, until finally, the return swing begins and in our old age we return back to the source. Terminology isn't very important here, so feel free to use being, God, consciousness, source, intelligence, energy, presence, or whatever you wish to describe your origins and identity.

Our function as adults is, instead of being the furthest away from our being and our true identity, to remain connected. Maybe we'll reach a point where we teach our children the truth in school, instead of loading their minds up with distortions of progress and competition. The truth is that our progress has come at a high cost. Our obsession and preoccupation with progress prevents us from realizing that there is already a part of us that is fully formed, perfect, and lacking absolutely nothing. Progress blinds us from experiencing the immediate reality. So long as modern man remains trapped by the quest for progress, he will remain blind to his own inherent perfection.

Our progress has had little influence over our inner laws. Outwardly it may look like we have made great strides, but if we look closer we will see that not only are we not progressing, but we have actually been falling into a deeper sleep. The answer is simplicity, independence, magnanimity, and trust. It is time to rise to heaven. Heaven is conceived as being above us, above the restless mind with its distortions of lack and suffering. We already have all of the solutions; we just need to be willing to implement them.

The first realization is to see that we live in a word that is unhinged. We can thank economic competition for getting us a nice house and a warm bed, but there is a better way to go about all of this. Our days don't have to be filled with unconscious sameness covering up our endless destruction. Everyone doing and saying the same things, the 9 to 5 job, the commute home, the same conversations with our friends and co-workers day in and day out. Where is our creativity and power? This isn't why we are here. How could the intelligence that created all of this possibly have that purpose in mind?

The truth is that we have no idea why we are here. We have given the world and our precious life experience here to something that isn't lasting. Our labels and concepts are wrong, and deep down we know they are simply misperceptions and stories, but we cling to and defend them to keep them alive because we're afraid of the truth. We fail to understand our own stories. Before we can heal, we must observe what we are feeding our minds, instead of arming ourselves with more well-intentioned beliefs and trying to fight the problem as if it had a reality outside of our current perception of it.

We think that we're here to accumulate, that stress is a necessary function, and that disease makes sense. But does it really? In whose eyes? Someone who is very mistaken. No reason that the thinking mind, or the ego, can possibly offer you for conforming to the lie is correct. And yet it will try; it will continue to poison your senses and obscure the truth until the fearful return swing begins.

But what is the solution on the material level. Is it more stuff? Better stuff? Even if we're surrounded by wonderful stuff, if we haven't yet grasped the truth of who we are, it will make us unhappy. Seeing something as good or bad, rich or poor, beautiful or ugly, is still just a belief that is subject to change based on our own personal mental states and sociocultural backgrounds. The truth we are pointing to here is not a fact that we must spend years studying and analyzing. It is a truth we can see all around us if we just learn to quiet our minds and see the obvious things which we never seem to observe.

At first, it might be scary to let go of our identities, no matter how horrible they may be, because without an identity, the mind will label the empty space as worthless. This shows us how very wrong the mind is that we listen to. The very source of life within us, our freedom and liberation, is labeled by our minds to be a place of darkness. And yet we know that the body is mostly empty space, and that the universe we find ourselves in is mostly empty, and the emptiest parts of it are the most powerful because they are filled with pure energy.

Life is a great paradox. The truth cannot be found in more facts or things, but only in emptiness. Emptiness is strength and power, it is heaven. It is a necessary prerequisite for the realization of truth and for the creation of any material reality.

Useless information, labels, and ideas are the bogus activities. Can we stop valuing them? Can we see the ugly truth of what they really are? Can we see our own egos? Can we laugh at the madness of our human drama?

The truth we've all heard in science class is that nothing can ever be created or destroyed. Perceptions can be created or destroyed, but not the truth. Our opinions can be created or destroyed, but not the life that we are. The inner, true part of us is completely innocent and at peace. It's the other part we've mistakenly chosen to identify with. The real part of us is invisible because it is formless, and yet it governs all form. Although invisible, it is hundreds of times more powerful. What we label as "real" are simply conditions perceived to be permanent due to the structure of our sense perceptions.

There is a part of us that is permanent, something we were given, something that isn't up to us. It is the temporary ego surrounding the soul that needs to be surrendered. We need to hand over our control. Our enemy (meaning our mechanical, unconscious tendencies) will continue to ask for seeming material strength, but if we dedicate our lives to such pursuits, it will lead to our eventual defeat. We don't need an army – all we need is inner surrender. We must transcend the limits of our own well intentioned, but deeply conceited attachment to the material world. Then, everything will be transformed. Nothing in this world will have the ability to sadden us. A reasonable mind can only take us so far, before we must abandon it and return to the unspoiled way of life.

Lesson 1: Today, you've chosen the truth. The false will be stripped away as you take back responsibility for your inner state. It is the first step toward freedom, and all you need to do is to remain open to whatever today brings. Remember that you are not the thoughts in your head.

CHAPTER 2

Experiencing Grace

Many enlightened people have said that our purpose is happiness. Does it make any sense that this is something that is outside of us, changes daily, and subjects us to struggle – when in fact we are the perceivers that create the material world? Would the wonderful intelligence that created us hold back our happiness until we had achieved some fleeting material goal? Happiness cannot be found in the outside world. Lasting happiness comes when we've discovered the truth of why we're here. What could bring us more joy than that?

No matter how many mistakes you think you've made, once you remember who you really are, you are forgiven, happy, and at peace. The ego that is currently running your mind is a monster because it does everything in its power to cover up and distort the truth. It is sad that we've listened to its madness for so long, but it is wonderful when we can finally awaken from this dream. This awakening is happiness. If it was up to the crazy mind with its self-invented personality, we would be trapped forever, born and conditioned to live here as slaves. It will try to trap us every step of the way, especially when awakening is attempted.

If we unconsciously believe in our conditioning, in everything our minds tell us, then we are no more than actors. No matter how good our roles might be, they are mechanical and can be observed; they don't have a material reality without our active participation.

Nothing seems real or alive because we're too attached to the conditions and roles we play. The zombie apocalypse has already happened and the cure is consciousness. There is nothing wrong with attachment, as long as it is filtered. Become attached to calmness and dispassion. In these states, awareness of bliss naturally occurs. Because we are human, it is part of our function to remain in this world; only now we choose to do so with a different level of consciousness. This is what Jesus meant when he said to be in the world but not of it. This takes an incredible degree of self-mastery, meaning freedom from the chains of our automatic thoughts and responses. To simply realize how very limited and automatic we are is the beginning of mastery, the beginning of the end of mechanical existence.

Our mind and our true nature is pure light. Spiritual awakening can be seen as realizing this abstract quality of pure light. We are no longer this or that because all such limited personal senses are gone. Fears of the future, as well as guilt, doubt, and everything else that isn't love, can be transcended. They may remain for a while, in which case, you will simply need to suffer through it. Remain humble, don't get discouraged. Remember that you are a spiritual pilgrim, embarking upon a great voyage. Of course it won't be easy and there will be setbacks, but do not fear. Even when you think that fear is most warranted, do not give into it, do not stop. The transcendence of fear is the most direct approach to enlightenment.

According to the Bhagavad Gita, each of us has three basic levels, from lowest to highest, which are sinner, active, and contemplative. A sinner is completely asleep, meaning that he is unconsciously run by the fears and limitations of the ego. This is our current world, the "devil" and "evil forces" are simply our misidentification with the material world, our experiment into creating with our egos. Then, in the active life, we are bettering ourselves through knowledge and doing, perhaps becoming successful in the eyes of the world. Eventually, the highest level is that of a contemplative, where we are able to fully surrender the self and realize that consciousness is the source of our supply and that we are simply the receivers of this divine gift. This level will look different to everyone. That's why not every enlightened person dresses and looks the same, and why even a "sinner" can achieve enlightenment because this perfect potential is already within each of us and all we have to do is to surrender the self, which means to stop thinking with the ego and allow consciousness to emerge.

True mastery is using our highest faculties to discern our current situation and thereby freeing ourselves from mechanical entrapment to both inner and outer conditions. Some teachings state that this world is an illusion, but we will not focus on that here. Our mission is not to deny, but to live more fully, breaking free every day and achieving true mastery.

Consciousness is the background which allows the thoughts, feelings, and sensations to be. Some people mistake consciousness for the mind, the thoughts that are you and yours. There is no such thing. Hinduism relates this as the horse, carriage, rider, and driver. The horse represents emotions which carry the carriage (your body) and rider (your sense of identity). The driver is the one who is responsible and aware of everything – and this is what is meant by consciousness. Most people are not awake enough to be aware of these centers, or to have a unified perception of their life. They don't possess direction or control because their thoughts and emotions are in constant conflict. They become angered and let it sweep them away instantly, because the emotions are allowed full control over the body since there are no filters in place.

Their thoughts and actions are no longer their own, their body is carried away with every fleeting sensation, but they don't realize how little control they have over themselves, and this is the main obstacle. When you don't realize you have a problem, you cannot begin to fix it. Although very limited, they believe themselves to be free and actually think that they choose to feel the way that they do.

Most spiritual teachers will tell you that you are here to allow the universe to unfold and that when you can submit to the will of God without any resistance, you will be reborn and your mind-made problems will disappear. But how can you get there? What does that mean? When you surrender your thoughts, aren't you just surrendering your identity? Can you really purify your mind and your life? Who will you be? Many people are so lost in their thoughts and emotions that they believe themselves to be victims of this world, and even though this identity is painful, they don't want to lose the only thing they know. Could your mental activity, which got you to this point, possibly have been wrong? If there was a better way to go about all of this, why didn't anyone tell you? And if this is the normal way of thinking, could we all be collectively wrong?

All suffering is created by mental activity which possesses you to identify with it by disguising itself as you. Suffering is the belief in a sick idea that isn't true because it comes from the voice of the ego. You unconsciously believe everything it says and react to all of its moods and emotions, because it is what you have been conditioned to believe and it happens inside your mind which makes you think that this is some personal phenomenon that you are responsible for. Your likes and dislikes were programmed by your ego at an early age, and liberation from this mind made prison seems almost impossible.

The thoughts of suffering, lack, and limitation which you believe to be your own are a part of the collective mind field which runs a vast majority of the population and creates similar circumstances and belief systems. In fact, as of right now, only a few people have achieved liberation from this. As human beings, most of us go through life completely unaware of the truth because we have been collectively domesticated by this insane voice. We believe that we are all human (material), and thus the being part of us (consciousness) isn't able to be heard.

So how do we free ourselves? We realize that if something such as the body doesn't have permanence, then it can't be the ultimate reality. Remember that life is a constant pendulum swing. Everything is in motion and nothing ever stops, yet most of us still find the concept of impermanence a difficult one to grasp, and thus we blindly believe that the impermanence around us is important and all-consuming. The seasons swing from summer to winter, the temperature swings from hot to cold, day to night, and even our emotions swing from love to hate. Our entire lives swing from life to death, and the fate of nations follows a similar trajectory, regardless of how we feel about it.

If nothing here is permanent, then who are we? Under the microscope, what is our real identity? Where will we go after this experience is over? Does it seem hard to believe that this body isn't who you really are? We say something is real if we can see it and touch it. And yet when we put it under a microscope, the "real" part of it disappears and we're left with mostly empty space, but this empty space is full of energy. We can start by accepting the fact that we have no idea what the word "real" means, or our current definition of it is just far too small.

It would seem that the only thing that is "real" is space, or emptiness, and our own cognitive ideation, which perceives and imagines our human world. We have never actually touched anything. Science gives us the example that if we were to isolate one atom and it was the size of an orange, the next closest atom would be two football fields away. It is almost unfathomable to think about how much space this is.

Lesson 2: You didn't pick your limited identity, and neither did anyone else. The only sane thing we can do now is to awaken together and to release our accumulated baggage. We are all connected, and as one evolves, the others follow.

CHAPTER 3

Imagination and Reason

When we refer to the ego, we're referring to the mental noise that creates our sense of who we are. This consists of our conditioned responses, as well as the things that we identify with in the physical world such as our jobs. The ego identity likes to think that it creates something worthwhile and that without its constant noise and manipulation, nothing would get done. The sad reality is that the reverse is true, and the very identity that you cling to is the thing that is creating the most unhappiness in your life. Only your true self, in its boundless freedom, can accomplish real creative work and peaceful existence because that is what you really are, and you can only manifest what you already are.

If you think you are small and limited, then you have forgotten who you really are. If you realign with the source, then you will manifest love and abundance in your life. You do have a mission and you are drawn to it with love. At the same time, you have another voice within you that tries to stop you, and unfortunately, most of the time it succeeds. You see the vast majority of the people around you struggling and you think it is almost selfish to be happy yourself. Struggle seems normal. Even the ultra-wealthy who have all the money in the world appear depressed. In a world accustomed to hardship, how can you be hopeful enough to believe in anything different?

It seems that everything that is born on this Earth must suffer. But the very fact that you have picked up this book means that you are brave enough, and that there is the intent within you to awaken in this lifetime, which is all you need. Your smallest intent will awaken deep forces within you which will help you along your spiritual path. You are a pilgrim returning from another land, a land of punishment and suffering, back to your true home.

Buddhism and Hinduism both believe the source of pain to be existence. Their doctrines teach that since birth exists, decrepitude and death ensue; for wherever there is a form, there is a cause for pain and suffering. Spirit alone has no form. The returning pilgrim, the evolved man, is one who more or less succeeds in freeing himself. Such a person lives as spirit.

We are held back from this realization by our own faulty reasoning and the negative thoughts that we harbor. But our lack of creativity can only take us so far, and we must abandon it if we wish to go further. We cling to it because we want an identity that can tether us in a shifting, frightful, and confusing world. Our strength, our energy, is used to fill involuntary and mostly negative aims. Can we take a leap of faith and release negative thoughts not only for the sake of our own happiness, but for the happiness of the world?

Can you imagine all the good that would come about if we weren't asleep, or completely identified with the ego, for the majority of the time? Remember that negative emotions and thoughts can only take you over when you're asleep. You didn't choose this identity; you were given it by a world that is mostly insane, with very little room left for doubt of any kind as to its benefits. Of course you can forgive yourself now for everything in the past because you were asleep, or infected with the disease of listening to the ego. None of it was the real you, and the same can be said for all other people. The real you wears no masks because it is pure love and joy and knows its true identity to be the observer and not the object being observed.

So, how do we stop negative thinking? Is it by cramming our minds with positive thinking dialogue? Any dialogue is a double edged sword, because it is part of the pendulum, and the direction can change in an instant. The real peace and joy that you are can't be expressed in words. It isn't a scripted dialogue tied to conditions and it can only be known in perfect stillness and faith.

The Buddhist way of stillness and meditation can be hard at first if you have a lot of inner pain you haven't dealt with, and many find it too abrupt of a change. A good start is through forgiveness, which is the first step toward higher consciousness. It is how we will move forward, and we know that we will because life loves to evolve. And who is here to experience life? Consciousness is the very life that you are and the realization of it is your gift. Of course you will realize it when you die and return to it, but to know it while you're alive is the biggest blessing. This is immortality because there is no longer the fear of death and the final illusion is transcended.

If you are currently harboring a grievance, the ego in you might send a thought such as, *How can I possibly forgive? I'm justified about this anger, I'm the victim.* When you forgive, you choose to stop identifying with the conditions of the outside world. You understand the actions taken by the other were done through misidentification and confusion due to the misuse of his or her faulty imagination. This is the first step toward compassion and understanding, and the noble use of your mind in releasing unpleasantness.

Your identity consists of the roles you've created and your mind will do anything to keep them. It loves the identity of the victim. But think about this for a moment: You unconsciously stepped into this identity, which has brought you problems and suffering. Is it possible that other people might have done the same? No one is to blame. We might call our belief in this small identity an illness. Most of us are suffering in some degree from this illness, which recognizes its smallness and weakness and therefore fights to destroy everything around it in order to strengthen its own identity.

The most beautiful energy source, which is who you really are, has chosen to cast itself in the awful role of your ego. It is almost as if we were living in some sort of freak experiment. If we want to create change and better the world, then we must cast off our current roles and most of what we have unconsciously allowed ourselves to believe. We must self-prescribe awakening, start filtering properly, and get down to the truth. We must use our imaginations and our reasoning faculties to create the good.

Let's now examine a modern example of a human life. F. Scott Fitzgerald was a great writer, full of enthusiasm, brilliance, knowledge, and tenderness. But apart from his great books, Fitzgerald's life was also full of struggle, sorrow, drinking, and ultimately an early death. Clearly, our mental states are subject to the same laws of the pendulum, and if we don't become aware of this, we will remain prisoners of this insane voice, the delusional one in our heads that never stops.

Fitzgerald's ability for great joy was coupled with his ability for great suffering. You cannot have one without the other. This is living in the pendulum, this is living on Earth. This is why many Christian authors have deemed human life to be full of vanities, and the Buddha deemed it to be full of suffering. The example we are trying to make here is that clearly, Fitzgerald was capable of feeling the absolute highs of life, and in so doing, was taken to the pains of the lows. This is the madness of our lives, the constant swing from enjoyment to suffering. Can we find the kind of happiness that has no opposite because it's not part of the pendulum? Judging by the smile of the Buddha, the words of Jesus, and the lives of enlightened people today, there is another kind of happiness that awaits us as we evolve and change the notions of what it means to be human.

On our journey home, we will undoubtedly be faced with highs and lows. The spiritual journey home is the journey to God, the invisible unknown that permeates everything we see around us. The human part of you can still experience the highs and the lows, but with a detached awareness that comes from realizing your own permanence or remembering your true home. This takes away all fear and you can play with the transitory nature of everything else around you because you no longer derive your sense of identity from it. You were meant to be a happy visitor here inside of your temporary body. You were never meant to believe that it is who you are, and all of the other mistaken notions that come along with it. Ultimately, nothing can really go wrong because all you are doing is experiencing life. Death is the return to the invisible realm and we cannot accurately describe it as bad. If you can intuitively understand this, then nothing can frighten you.

It is said that before the Buddha achieved enlightenment he felt as if every bone of his body was breaking. Before a journey ends, it is prefaced with a dark night in which you are torn apart both internally and externally, but if you keep going, then your greatest reward lies immediately beyond the passage of this final threshold, the one that so few are ever able to cross. It is written in the Bible that during Jesus' last night on Earth, in the Garden of Gethsemane, "And being in anguish, he prayed more earnestly, and his sweat was like drops of blood falling to the ground."[1]

I'm sure you've heard it said that it's always darkest before the dawn, and if things seem really bad, then most likely they will get much better soon. The spiritual journey isn't an easy one. There must be sufficient pain in order to force you to evolve, otherwise you would be trapped in the temporarily pleasant but empty life as a regular human. Suffering can be used as a tool to transcend the current limitations of the body, and this can only be done when you face your fears.

Lesson 3: Anything that isn't love today, simply watch it and walk past it. Free your mind from the burdens of mechanical existence and restore yourself to your original vastness.

CHAPTER 4

The Treasure

If we take a moment to think about it, what is our world? It's a little ball floating in the middle of nothing. Everything is empty space, or pure energy without form. Our human life consists mostly of fighting empty space, stillness, and silence. The only real way to get anywhere is to awaken, and this is what we are destined for.

The men who founded America were very radical thinkers. Imagine, coming from a place where you were ruled by a king, but deciding to start over in a whole new land, with a limited government, and to believe that every man, under God, was entitled to happiness. Let's not forget the fact that early America had a very small army and little support and that no rebellion had ever been successful against such a large colonial empire as England. The very fact that God and happiness are mentioned in the Constitution shows that the founding fathers were inspired. George Washington stepped away from the presidency after only two terms and told his fellows that they must not be thinking clearly if they wanted him to stay for yet another term. He believed that every man should be in charge of himself, and to put that power in the hands of anyone else would only bring trouble.

Yet somewhere down the line, the freedom of the founding fathers turned into the greed of their successors. Their wishes were thrown away as America set up its first central bank. The founding fathers were against such notions and Thomas Jefferson believed that banking institutions were more dangerous than standing armies. Then Meyer Amschel Rothschild came along and created a system from which the Rothschild banking dynasty could become the wealthiest family in human history. The system of lending is based upon amassing fortunes from unearned profit by collecting interest on debt. So long as a system like this exists, based on a maldistribution of wealth and an endless circulation of borrowing principal and consequently creating more debt that can never be repaid, no country can be truly free.

 From the moment the Federal Reserve was created, all currency would enter circulation as a loan on interest. The founding fathers understood this, which is why they were so against centralized banking. There are men now running America and profiting immeasurably and they want nothing more than to control and keep this system of deceit, struggle, and subversion alive.

And yet we continue to believe that we are somehow part of a system that finds us capable and deserving of health, wealth, and happiness. In reality, this system robs us of our chief duty, our birthright for prosperity.

Currently, our entire system of economics is not worthy of the name because there is nothing economical about it. There is ultimately no net profit, nothing good being produced in any large number. If we continue to engage in a system which centers on the very thing which does not work, we cannot hope for a better future. We must be honest with ourselves and realize that there is no true profit here; that our current system actually deprives us of economy.

No solutions are available on the news because the news is yet another medium for this unconsciousness. We watch two hours of footage about an event, and at this event nothing new is discussed and no action is ultimately taken and it goes on and on in an endless cycle. It is all used to blind us and occupy our minds; keep us asleep. But we were not born to remain unconscious. The truly sad part is that the majority of participants in this system have no idea what they are participating in, and yet every day they add to the continuing dominance of the current state of affairs.

Let's take a look at the world now. At the workplace we smile with clenched teeth as we say to one another, *Have a nice day!* During our commutes, we refuse to make eye contact with other drivers. Our self-imposed isolation prevents us from connecting with others and is actually beneficial for our current economy because it puts us in perpetual competition and separation. Our solution is to join together, but we cannot currently do so, and so we feel alone and become overwhelmed with ourselves.

When we finally do get home or wherever it is we're headed to in such a hurry, there is no relief. We must look forward to yet another moment because this one is usually unacceptable. We watch ads for medications which we self-prescribe because we have no idea how to function in this world. At what point do we decide to stop working for a profit that doesn't profit us – a system based on the dispossession of our intrinsic human rights?

The solution is not a mathematical treatise or an economic formula; it is simply coming together, unifying, supporting, and loving one-another and the organic life that supports and sustains us. It is creating love within our families and workplaces. It is a revolution similar to the one that America had in its infancy, only this time it's a little harder because we are not yet fully aware of the decrepitude to which we subject ourselves. In early America the madness was easily seen in unjust taxation, lack of representation, and other affronts to civil liberties. This time, although we feel the hurt within ourselves, we are still blinded by the apparent progress which we think we are making in our free economy. We must stop wasting our precious life energy in competition and conflict with one another because that only supports our current madness.

We think we have to struggle for money and struggle to survive, and our educational systems are ready to prepare us for this struggle – we are deceived from the very start. We have fallen asleep and have allowed our wealth to fall into the undeserved hands of a select few. It is madness. And it is also time to begin the awakening process. When we choose love and peace we are choosing to leave this world and enter the heavenly realm, because love and peace are not of this world. It is our function to bring them here.

Eventually our system of debt will end because we will run out of the necessary resources to service it. There will simply be too much of it to manage, and we will look for a different way. We will unite in our desire toward peace and justice for everyone on Earth. When we understand that our current economy is based upon usury, or the undeserved accumulation of wealth due to the unceasing circulation of debt, we can then choose to return to a simpler way of living. The obvious faults of our world will never be solved with our current system. The fact that we have been unconscious for so long, and have believed in this system, and continue to fight to protect it, goes to show you just how deeply deceptive it is and how well it is able to turn us against ourselves.

Politicians understand this problem and they add to it with every inconsiderable detail and never mention the true root of everything that is wrong with our current world. It is the outward manifestation of the darkest desires of the human mind, the ego, and it tries to go by the name of progress, civilization, and economics. Debt is never free and cannot exist in a truly free economy because debt and freedom are two mutually exclusive concepts. Only a free mind can create a free economy; people who are armed with the stark perception of truth and knowledge and no longer brainwashed by the world.

The current system is presently setting itself up to keep us asleep forever, and the only way to stop it is to demand a system that will actually serve *us*, instead of the other way around, and we are now at the beginning of the end. We are waking up. We realize that we are part of a system which takes our money and uses it for its own profit and speculation. When Andrew Jackson ended the charter of the Second Bank of the United States in 1834, he warned us about our current state of affairs. He said that when the current system wins, it divides the profit amongst the select hands of the few. When it loses, it charges that loss to all of us, thereby ensuring that it never fails and we never profit.

In the present day this is evident if you step into an investment firm or turn on CNBC and listen to their dialogue, which goes along the lines of, "Why is the market up so high? Oh, it's because the unemployment numbers came out." Actual unemployment doesn't matter, but someone's *interpretation* of unemployment numbers and whether or not they look good does. Actual unemployment can be readily seen, just look at the people who aren't working and the impact that their lack of production is having on the economy. But this is where the trap lies –actual production is impossible to track and is even unnecessary because we have moved away from physical production and physical goods to an economy that makes money by moving money.

Most physical production has been outsourced to other countries. This is the type of complexity that the current system needs. They don't need us to be employed or unemployed, all they need to do is to speculate and move money around so that they can profit. When the numbers come out, someone makes a decision about what this data means and their speculation drives the markets, causing millions of people to gain or lose money at the drop of a hat. Money is moved according to the ideas of a select few, based on how they feel about employment or unemployment, currency, what a firm is doing, what a leader is doing, or what they think a foreign country might or might not do fifty years from now. Upon closer examination their speculations have no rational basis. It is a system based upon their opinions and it generates billions of dollars per year for them, while impoverishing millions of others and sharing only a minute fraction of its profits.

Thoreau (living in the same time period as Andrew Jackson and the brief demolishing of the bank) gave an example in *Walden* of the overlooked benefits of the simple, wild, or savage tribal state. He quoted a man who lived with a savage tribe in Africa. At night time, sitting around the fire, they would let the civilized white visitors sit close to it and still the white people were shivering. The tribe sat far away but was actually sweating from all the heat. How could there be such a difference between the tribal people and the civilized? Thoreau said it was because in the tribe they kept their inner flame alive, and in the civilized world, we have given our inner flame away and must rely on an outer fire to keep us warm. We have become expert delegators, subjecting ourselves to the mercy of fleeting conditions. This is very dangerous and it is the very thing that George Washington warned against. Most of us don't know how to build our own dwellings or provide our own food and our schools do nothing to correct this. By relying on so many outer conditions, and constantly giving away our power, we unknowingly become more unconscious every day. We accept it out of convenience, and end up surrendering something which was perhaps much more useful.

In a universe that is abundant and perfect, how can it be that the most advanced life form is the most limited? How can the entire universe run perfectly for billions of years, but we can't get even the brief 80 or 100 years that each of us is here right? Could divine order and love have missed humans so completely? And if we aren't run by life, what are we run by? Something that is very counter to it and something that humans have created, which is delusion, or ego.

We have no heavenly treasure here in the form of peace or love, and the tragic thing is that these treasures are the only ones that matter. Although we have improved our outer conditions, unfortunately, this progress did not come with any sort of improvement to our inner lives. We are no more spiritually advanced, no happier, than we were 100 years ago, and the argument could be made that we are now even less so. We must take a closer look at civilization and at all the useless facts which we have used to better domesticate ourselves.

Civilized life has many things in common with death. Death means that we have no ability to respond to life, we feel helpless. Why do we give ourselves up for the scraps of false comfort?

So, what is important? If we know that someday this form will disappear, what do we want to do with this temporary experience? If we realize that our actual size in relation to the size of the universe is smaller than a grain of sand, how much can we really claim to know? Can we yield and be willing to learn and to enjoy ourselves and all the love that surrounds us? Or do we want to keep creating chaos and thinking that we have it all figured out? The time has come when enough of us can stop and see the world we have created for what it really is.

Pondering our existence will no longer be an elevated topic, reserved only for a select few; it will reclaim its place as our most elementary need. When we focus on self-actualization, we focus on right-action and peace, on the ultimate fulfillment of our destinies. When we get this part right, then all of the other needs such as physiological, safety, love, and esteem will all fall into place. Our main error lies in the pursuit of all these other needs first, without giving care to the proper foundation. Very few of us ever reach full self-actualization, and we reach it after much struggle in the outer world. This is inverted and needs to be corrected if we truly wish to achieve any of the other comforts such as love and safety. Morality, creativity, and spirituality must come first.

The Russian author, Fyodor Dostoyevsky, who wrote such classics as *The Brothers Karamazov, Crime and Punishment*, and *The Idiot*, also stressed a compassionate view toward life. The title of his book, *The Idiot*, can be misleading for the very reasons we are expounding here. Namely, that an ego-refusing person is *improperly* regarded as an "idiot" by his fellow humans. Dostoyevsky, much like Thoreau and Lao Tzu, urged us to get back to honesty and simplicity. He urged us to love the animals, plants, and everything around us. Such a state would naturally allow for us to perceive the divine mystery of life.

As Thoreau wrote, we build our lives around our fancy homes and clothes, but before we pursue such outer luxuries, we should focus on making our inner lives beautiful. Once we perfect and simplify the inner self, we can live a truly rich and refined life, but it cannot be the other way around. The trappings of outer life will not provide true and everlasting beauty and peace. We should focus on perfecting the inner self, decorating and upgrading within. We must open ourselves up to find the truth, or at least be open to receiving the truth when it is laid down upon our doorstep.

A life without spiritual richness and inner work is empty. Although surrounded by beautiful things, without fostering the spiritual faculty within, such a life remains half dead. We must make ourselves beautiful again so that everything can reflect our beauty. There is nothing wrong with beautiful homes and possessions, but there is something wrong when the people living inside are not focused on their own spiritual evolution and self-mastery. Our life will once again return to its predestined grandeur once we are willing to sacrifice our superficial comforts and act with greater intelligence.

The ordinary objects of human luxury, such as property and outward success, are ultimately empty. We are calling for a revolution, but not one that overthrows anything in the outer world. This is an inner, spiritual transformation, taken on by each of us as individuals. We must become skeptical of what we have thus far labeled as *progress*. This is a mental path that we need to embark upon so that we can be healthy again and connect the visible and invisible parts of ourselves; our higher nature and our material nature.

Presently, we believe that we must first focus on the physical needs before we can focus on reaching our full potential. This is to be expected since we live in a world that so heavily focuses on the physical and doesn't understand the direct relationship between the mental and physical worlds. If we understood that our mental states produced our physical states, then of course we would all choose to focus on self-actualization. Focusing on food or sex would seem like madness if we truly knew what was important. This is also why the lives of Buddha and Jesus are so fascinating – because they let go of their so-called primary needs (such as home and food) and focused fully on the higher states and reaching man's full potential.

We have inner needs, and there is nothing in our outer world that will fulfill these needs, and as long as they remain unmet, we will remain unsatisfied. This inner fulfillment is our primary task and it will naturally lead us toward solutions for all of our perceived difficulties. Such growth will foster a change of consciousness, but in order to get there, we must be open to the fact that there is more to the universe than what is apparent to our senses. We must not accept our current level of interpretation as final.

As it has often been said, the first step toward inner growth begins with present moment awareness. This requires a radical level of simplicity. The outer world will continue to throw impulses our way, but we must move beyond the noise in order to reach a level which we have not known thus far. This is our source. This is where we go before birth and death, and during the night when we close our eyes.

The point of being in the present moment is to distance ourselves from the material world. Watch past moments and future anxieties. Perform your actions with detached, heightened awareness, and know that you are none of the transitory things around you. Then you will begin to move slowly up the levels of consciousness and understanding until you reach full realization of the truth. With this state, all fear dissolves. When the body becomes old, you are peacefully able to leave it and return to your true self, which is consciousness, or part of God.

Our modern human history isn't a mere 6,000 years as some would have you believe. It is millions of years, with many years of consciousness followed by unconsciousness (belief that you are living apart from God – where we are currently) and back to consciousness, in between. We have only recently re-discovered that we are energy.

Ultimately, there is nothing to do. Of course there is the life that you live and the tasks that you do with your body on a daily basis. But now, these activities will be realized as small things. They will no longer take all of your attention and force you into either great ecstasy or despair. You will enjoy the play of form all around you and remain connected with your source. All striving and seeking will end and you will be able to live your life day by day with ease. At least this is the intended plan. Some may be able to reach it in this lifetime, and others will continue to stay trapped in the ego, only to be liberated later on.

God is the doer, or the performer of all action. Everything is God and you are a temporary single manifestation of God. This is why so many great saints and sages of the past have said to love everything and to see God in everything. You realize that you are consciousness, and that this experience on Earth is merely energy creating matter.

When you have a desire and it is fulfilled, you know that it was consciousness acting through you. When you have a desire that isn't fulfilled, that too is consciousness acting through you. The world is at a level of perfection which is beyond human understanding, and you naturally find the seed of bliss in every circumstance.

St Therese of Lisieux, born in 1873, who was called one of the greatest saints of modern times, said she used to wonder why this gift of grace was not equally bestowed upon everyone. She wondered why God didn't pick those who are "worthy", but those he chose. Such preference and seeming inequality baffled her. She finally came to the realization that we are all like little flowers, different, but playing important roles in the garden. Life loves variety and we will never be able to fully understand why it is the way that it is.

Let's take a modern example of how a shift in consciousness can change your life. I once read about a rock climber who was passionate and adventurous. However, his week was full of commuting and working long hours in advertising. He was being drawn to a specific climbing area, so he decided to take a leap of faith and leave the corporate world to develop it. He followed his calling, and soon the world gave him a new identity. He was asked to be the head of a team that protects the natural climbing areas of the very place he felt happiest being.

We are all being mysteriously drawn to our divine mission here on

Earth. We are here to serve and to make a difference. Following our heart takes a leap of faith, but if we are willing, the universe will be there to help and guide us. Our passions are within us for a reason, so long as we are willing to take action.

The spiritual quest is similar to climbing a very tall rock without any rope for protection. Once you make it past the halfway mark, meaning that you are too high to jump back down safely, there is really only one option left: keep climbing to the top and finish what you started, no matter how terrifying it might be. Once you begin pondering spiritual truths, they will never leave you; your life will be forever changed as you begin to awaken. You will look at everything differently, and it might be terrifying, because your simple change in perception will alter your entire life.

Lesson 4: Today, remember that limits are completely mental. It's all about belief. And remember that you already have everything within you. You don't have to be impeccable. Simply focus on letting go of as much negativity as you can.

CHAPTER 5

Compassion

Can we work together to create a society where all are allowed and encouraged to be free and happy and follow their true purpose? Can we pass by someone and notice the pain in his eyes, instead of being absorbed with ourselves, and then choose to offer him some of our strength and joy? Such a gift brings blessings to the entire world and it's an easy choice to make. It is only the ego that has us trapped and thinking that the way things are now is the best they can be.

We are meant to help one another so that we can all be happy. We are all meant to live and enjoy the world in every moment. As long as there is one of us that still believes in suffering, he is asleep, and we cannot reach our full potential until we are all awake. Like a team, we don't finish the race until the slowest among us has crossed the finish line. This slowest one is trying to bring his house, possessions, and all of the other things he thinks make him who he is with him on his back and they are slowing him down. He's almost completely tethered to the ground under the weight of unnecessary things and false identification. He needs your help to let them go and cross the finish line as a free man in full realization of who he is. Then, as soon as this happens and the heaviest-laden among us has realized his true identity, we will all evolve into higher levels of consciousness. This is sanity and success and this is what planet Earth is destined for.

Some of us are ready to evolve now. Others don't realize that humans need to evolve because they think we are already the absolute best that we can be. Seen in this light, we can begin to question the authority we've crowned. How did we let the most confused among us lead us for so long?

Life is a beautiful, magical gift, so how does any pursuit other than spiritual make any sense? Let's not forget the higher state and our tremendous potential for a heavenly life. Great art is an expression of heaven – let's not use it to domesticate ourselves. Let's stop being comfortable with only an earthly existence. This is the inspiration each of us has within and we can no longer afford to silence it. We know too much to remain asleep.

Everyone has yin and yang aspects, or opposite forces that interconnect. There doesn't need to be a constant struggle between the soul and the intellect. This chapter is an appeal to the yang in all of us, which is the masculine/action part. Yin is silent and feminine. Once we are silent and centered (yin), we can act (yang) with truth because both are equally important. We are here to act and to expand, but we must learn to do so beautifully and wisely, to create the perfect balance of yin and yang. This will require hard introspection and truthful self-analysis.

Why did we allow ourselves to believe that we are here to do jobs that we don't love while we struggle with our health, relationships, and finances? Even those who are blessed to have jobs they love must still overcome the struggle of working with the unconscious people around them. And even the most successful people among us, the celebrities and politicians, after they have reached the limits of material success, often realize that they know nothing about the true meaning of life.

In tribes, no one goes hungry. Everyone gets a house. No one is told to work until he is exhausted. No one is told to struggle. What is it exactly about modern civilization that we find so appealing? Our progress could have taken us to a place where there is wealth equality, free medical care, and adequate food. But we decided to measure progress in other ways. Our desire for false wealth has taken us away from the truth, and any time we travel away from the truth, we create suffering for ourselves and the world around us. We create separation and competition and this division is what fuels the ego.

Many people feel trapped in their current perception of reality, and this creates isolation and dissatisfaction. They have become disillusioned with the world because they have forgotten that they have the power of intention. With intention, we can decide to create. Then, with responsibility, we can choose our reaction to life; we are no longer mechanically responding to the conditions of the world, completely run by the mind and emotions. If we are truly made in the image and likeness of God, can we not keep these small commandments for his sake? Suffering and desperation come about from a heavy inner state, but through responsibility and intention, we can release them and take back our power.

We all want the vital, unlimited freedom that was destined for us. Our current institutions will not give it to us, and it is up to us to create it for ourselves. As soon as we desire intention and responsibility in our lives, we will begin to harness our inner fires and life will begin working with us and for us. After many years spent living as victims, this is the most vital step for us to take.

At first, it may not seem easy. In fact, since this other side of reality is so unknown to us, it may be terribly painful to dwell in peace for any length of time because our intellect will feel starved and uncomfortable. Problems are the meat which our current intellect needs to thrive. But instead of running away from this discomfort, remember that you are a warrior, or to use a more modest term, a pilgrim. You are a newcomer attempting to discover a distant land, a separate reality within yourself, and ready to fight if you must. Let your intellect and your ego feel uncomfortable. Take pride in starving out the false. There is no harm in this, only long-term good.

Your intellect is right because there will be nothing you can explain. You are drifting in the middle of an ocean, and from where are you now, you can see both shores: your illusory world, and your true home. Both seem equally appealing for the simple fact that they are solid land, but since you decided to take this journey, for the time being, you are not a part of any land. You are drifting, floating, and it may not be comfortable. But comfort is a heavy delight that you will need to abandon.

Most of us are beginners on the spiritual path, meaning that we still struggle with attachment to thought. Choosing to step away, to watch, is not an easy step to make. This radical detachment, a simple observation of inner phenomenon, as if your thoughts weren't even you, isn't as easy as it sounds. But the unconscious is something you must watch with non-reaction, and don't take anything personally.

Forgive, let go, and this will lead you to the truth. Truth isn't something you learn on Earth. Unfortunately very little truth is taught in the world. The only way you can get the truth is by allowing it to come to you. It is a heavenly gift and the only thing it asks of you is just to open yourself up to receive it. Remember that you are the divine child of a loving creator. This is your higher self, and it can only be heard when you silence your mind and let go of your notions of guilt and suffering. You are perfect, whole, and complete right in this moment.

It is said that the Buddha, upon his enlightenment, cried out, "Wonder of wonders! Intrinsically all living beings are Buddhas, endowed with wisdom and virtue, but because people's minds have become inverted through delusive thinking they fail to perceive this." Enlightenment is the realization that you are perfect already. Lao Tzu wrote that, "Because clarity and enlightenment are within your own nature, they are regained without moving an inch." You must forgive yourself and everyone, and let go of the thoughts constantly running through your mind.

Stop identifying with the ego and die to the small self with all its rules and tension. It has often been said by all of the religions in one way or another: Unless we die, we cannot be born again. Rumi and Jesus both spoke of a death that takes place while we're still alive. This is the death of our ego identities, our unconscious tendencies toward suffering and limitation. This death will be the harbinger of peace, a symbol that we are ready to receive our promised salvation, and to be transformed into a new race of humans.

"Forgive them for they know not what they do." Jesus realized that the people around him were unconscious. They were cut off from the source and when that happens, the only way to label it is tragic. The truth is that we must either collectively evolve or we will continue to destroy until all is dead. A few of us waking up here and there simply isn't enough anymore. This is a call to action on the grandest scale. Both yin and yang will come together and we will be peaceful and powerful. We will be what God intended us to be and it will be heaven on earth. We will once again begin to see clearly as our two worlds, the earthly and the heavenly, meet. Now, many years later, enough people might finally be ready in order to fully awaken the entire world. We are all part of a collective organism that is connected at every level. Once a critical number of us are able to awaken, it will become easier for others to follow. This is also why so many of us are suffering right now. Before such an awakening, the ego will try whatever it can in order to prevent it, and as long as there is pain, we will all feel it at some level.

When you are connected with the truth your inner flame burns brightly and all of your bodily systems are flooded with energy. When you are disconnected, you extinguish this vital life flame within you through useless thinking and negativity. Imagine how much more energy you'd have if you could stop thinking about the past and the future and concentrate on the present moment. Stop wasting your life energy on imaginary conversations and situations which may or may not happen. If they happen, great. If they don't happen, it doesn't really matter.

Nothing can ever be created or destroyed. That goes for energy as well. Bad or destructive energy, meaning ego, can only be transformed back into consciousness. Redirect your anger and transform it into the fuel of your spiritual aspirations. This is why it is said that darkness disappears in the light. The billionaire Elon Musk, creator of SpaceX and Tesla, said that he had a major revelation as a child when he realized that darkness in itself was simply the absence of light. All fear of the dark disappeared for him in that moment.

The Bhagavad Gita states, "That which is unreal does not exist. That which is real cannot cease to exist." A Course in Miracles puts it this way, "Nothing real can be threatened. Nothing unreal exists. Herein lies the peace of God." You must align yourself with the real. Don't fight the darkness, because it cannot be destroyed – it can only be observed and transformed.

Jesus was able to respond with love and compassion in the midst of great evil and suffering. When we are connected to the source we function with effortless grace, power, and self-worth, no matter the circumstances. We make the world a better place simply with our presence. We are able to bring love to everyone and everything around us. We never abuse ourselves or others. We love the simple things, like nature and animals and even in the midst of illness we are able to live with poise and tranquility and bring only love into the world.

Lesson 5: Today, focus on finding the truth within. Remember that the natural state of life is one of beauty, creativity, bliss, and abundance. Focus on truth, and let everything else take care of itself.

CHAPTER 6

The Primitive Condition and the Higher State

Our main illusion is that we think we are limited in two key areas: power and peace. Without these two things, it is impossible to live happily. If we didn't innately possess these two faculties, if only a handful of people on Earth were able to snag them, we would all be in trouble indeed, and struggle and depression would certainly be warranted. Luckily, that's not the case.

We have unlimited power and we can remain peaceful no matter what situation is in front of us. The only thing we need to do is take back control of our minds in the form of the mind training we're doing now. We have remained primitive thus far, making little progress in our spiritual work. Now is the time to rise to our higher states. As of yet, only a brave few have been able to lift the veil of darkness from the world and to achieve the highest expressions of character and personality.

Spiritual health begins when we realize that our identity isn't a body here on Earth, but spirit. This will lead us to our real self, which is joy, peace, and happiness. These are states that cannot be learned here because they are not from here; they must be remembered because they are a part of us.

When your consciousness expands, you feel like things slow down. And yet, you function at speeds that greatly surpass the unconscious mind which is frantically scrambling about. You don't focus on the tiny details of personality and you become vast, empty, clear, and powerful. This clarity lets you bypass all of the unnecessary mental noise and interruption – which are states that most people live in. They get stuck in the smallness of life while you can soar above it with the gift of mental clarity.

In the unconscious mind, meaning the state that hasn't yet experienced the work of self-mastery, there is a constant battle against the conditions of life due to the fixation on the outer world. There is never any flow or harmony, and energy is wasted ceaselessly. However, if we are tired of this, we can embark upon the grueling work of freeing ourselves. Thus far, we have trudged very deeply off the path and each step back may be painful. However, if we do the necessary work, once we reach the path again, the higher state within us will shine forth and provide the necessary direction and clarity. When we're on the path, the struggles of character don't concern us anymore. When we busy our minds with struggle, we are traveling on wild ground with its many bumps, turns, and delays because we are only able to see a few feet in front of us. Our salvation is silence – meaning freedom from the small stories that get us stuck in the muck. This is all enlightenment is.

If you focus on every second of your life, you can't help but to become lighthearted. Everything feels strange, alive, and fresh, because it is no longer filtered through recycled labels of the mind. You are on a clear path and the walking is easy. There is no mud to fight against or bushes to clear.

How do you get to this state? Love everything you see around you at this moment, because then you are choosing to believe in the part of you that comes from consciousness, instead of the ego which comes from Earth and which has very precise requirements for happiness. Expand and awaken. You are not a victim; you are the very source of life itself. The greatest gift is within you and you are the only one who can realize it. You are meant to find it within yourself, and this is actually your only goal, no matter if you are aware of it or not. As it has often been said, die while you're alive, and shed the old identity. Otherwise, what would be the point?

The world that surrounds you is a beautiful game of forms, but don't get lost in it. Be still and feel the joy that is within you. It is life. There is no work or stress that you must put yourself through in order to experience it. Perhaps this is why it has eluded so many people. It is a letting go, a surrendering of all the "progress" you've made up to this point and replacing it with an openness to receive a heavenly gift. Remember that struggle is of the ego, and consciousness is a return to spirit. You can make this return while you continue to inhabit your human identity. This is mastery of life.

In truth, this world is magnificent. In January of 1984 my great grandmother passed away. Before going to bed she stood by her window looking out at the fallen snow. She said "The world is so beautiful I don't want to leave it." She passed away quietly that night. No one knows how much time you'll have here so choose wisely. Choose consciously. There is a way to love the world, to be happy, to be here, and to participate, while at the same time to not be afraid of it. To appreciate it and to have no fear of what will come after your time here is done. This is the beautiful mystery we need to be comfortable with because we are made of it.

Taking this step isn't easy. You must have become tired enough of your old identity in order to seek the truth. Just like the parable that Jesus relates of the lost son who has squandered all of his wealth and finally decides to return to God his Father. Not only does his Father welcome him, but they both love each other even more than before. There is an added depth that his journey has given him. But only when he had squandered all of his riches, meaning he had nothing left in the world of form and was in great suffering, was he able to return to his Father.

Buddhist master Trungpa Rinpoche said that to be a spiritual warrior, one must have a broken heart. Maybe suffering has brought you here and you've squandered enough of your worldly wealth and seek to return home. Maybe you've realized at some level that nothing you see around you is permanent, and that none of it can possibly add to the true sense of who you are. Maybe your home life or work life has shown you the unreality of it all and you're ready to discover your true purpose. The old, completely unconscious patterns of your mind did serve a purpose. All life is here to evolve and to grow in tune to whatever action you take because you impact all life everywhere.

The mind is a trap and it will grab you with all of its labels. If you are just starting the awakening process, for a while you will continue to believe that this destructive process is actually trying to protect you. Your ego is a bold spear and if you aren't conscious enough you might find yourself destroying the very thing which you seek.

All of the great scriptures have told us this in one way or another, Jesus spoke of surrender while Buddha spoke of emptiness. Jesus said, "Whoever wants to be my disciple must deny themselves and take up their cross and follow me."[1] How can we ignore the truth the way that we do? This is where an almost angry determination can come in, a desperate desire to awaken from this dream and to gain control over our lives. We no longer wish to play out these roles, but as of yet we cannot see a way out. And the horror is that we are still living in this nightmare, only now we realize that we have a choice to awaken, and we wish to do so as soon as possible because the old dream is becoming unbearable.

Don't worry, eventually the momentum of useless thinking will stop. You will finally feel at peace and realize that this was your true identity all along. Nothing in the world can adequately describe the indescribable. It will never fit completely into the confines of our limited language. It takes great boldness to be this simple and to allow ourselves to be led to luminous emptiness. Boehme, the Christian mystic and theologian, believed that we could come into a new reality of our being and perceive everything in a new relation if we could simply stand still and separate ourselves from our constant self-thinking.

While driving I've often noticed "Do not block" signs at intersections. When we cling to something, we stop the natural flow of life. We block and everything becomes congested. We must realize that everything has a stage of birth, death, and new birth, and we must become comfortable with simply experiencing it all.

Lesson 6: When we cling to something for our sense of identity, we stop the flow. Today, stop clinging to labels. Let them expire and replace them with the truth of whatever the present moment holds.

CHAPTER 7

I am a Visitor Here

The language we've been given feels limited, at best. Is there any other way to communicate and see people? I think so. When you pay enough attention to the natural world, you'll notice that it is all listening to a mysterious automatic process that functions without any language that is known to us. But what if we could learn this process and speak its language instead? Could this be the true language of life? It's clear that our own process, which is strictly linear, doesn't compare since we've only been able to understand a small fraction of the life around us. Even 1,000 years from now we will still be busy trying to figure out how the human body works.

For some, this type of view may be too far removed and they worry that if they surrender some of the mental talk and roles that the mind has created, it will be insensitive and the relationships they've learned to cherish might suffer. And yet, here is the great paradox. Only by viewing others with the quiet language of nature, as spirit to spirit, can we honor their presence. There are no right words that the roles we play can possibly give us if we don't simultaneously connect with the part of us that has no language. Everyone wants to be recognized as the life that he or she is, not simply the temporary role-play or dialogue. In the spiritual world this is referred to as the one within the many.

We play temporary roles which evolve from child, to adult, to parent, to grandparent. But there is a deeper one life that is within us all. This is the true language. When you can become still enough to recognize this presence within you, you will usually find that the desire to use words diminishes. You'll see that words belong to an outer world which was never the true part of you. You'll see that the truth is within, part of the invisibility that forms itself into something, becomes something. But this something can never give you true fulfillment. What you really need cannot be found out there, and it is essential for us to realize that our senses do not hold the key to our happiness, and that actually quite the reverse is true. A living death, a numbing of our mechanical bodily sense perceptions, is needed so that we can once again start moving in the right direction, to the place before the body.

It's enough to just feel the love that is within as you interact with everyone that you happen to meet in your life. Even as your roles change, you are rooted in your true identity, and thus the suffering stops. This comes from not placing any blame or unconsciousness on anyone and remaining awake in the world. In this way, you can reveal your true perfect nature and simultaneously help others to remember theirs. Can you imagine what life will be like when we stop treating one another like some fact machines that need to be programmed and domesticated in every way possible for the brief and limited period of time that we're here? If we remain unconscious, we will continue taking the joy of being alive right out of life. The good news is that the solution is very simple: Let the crazy stories die. Trust life to kill your old identity.

At first, periods of awakening may be brief and you might still catch thoughts in your mind about the past (usually bad events) and about the future (again usually bad events). You might make plans for yourself and your family and career but if you aren't careful, these plans and conditions will begin to cause stress. Whenever that happens, you must realize that you've put too much emphasis on them. You must become diligent and filter your mind.

When we leave this world, will we take any of our plans or achievements with us? No. The only thing that will be coming with us is the thing that was never born and will never die. Don't let it be covered up with temporary roles, scripts, and opinions. Being human is an exploration and a deep experiment which baffles us. Once our time here is done, we will return to the place from which we came. Let's stop pretending we already know the most important parts of life. Instead, let's strive to catch even a small glimpse of the big picture, through unknowing the false, before the time of earthly death. When the body is able to correctly identify itself, this is the true fulfillment of its purpose.

When you are connected with the life within you, you are able to forgive yourself for moments of unconsciousness. You realize it was a temporary role you decided to inhabit, and not an eternal truth. You no longer want to make the false, scripted role the truth for you. You take away the power and momentum of unconsciousness. There are some people who are so identified with their current roles on Earth that they've lost all connectedness to the truth and the life within them. These are the people with strong opinions and ego identities. They harbor a lot of guilt and pain and find it very hard to forgive. It is important to be careful and patient because their ego will try to pull you in to identifying with it as well. Then, if you get upset, you are only strengthening their attachment to what is false in them, and planting that seed in yourself as well.

Lao Tzu said that any anger is a departure from the truth. We are here to free one another from these roles and it all starts with forgiveness. Forgiveness can only come from connecting with the life within you and seeing it as the truth both in yourself and others. Then, the outside game of form is able to continue but with the love and peace that it was intended to. Know that every relationship was given to you so that you could choose to learn. This is why many people refer to life as a school.

We frantically throw roles at ourselves and others and get upset when we or they don't comply. Unhappiness comes because life isn't going the way we think it should. As Alanis Morissette sings, "... I'm a lover, I'm a child, I'm a mother, I'm a sinner, I'm a saint..." If we remain asleep, we will believe all these different roles are who we really are. We will be in constant stress and turmoil because no matter how perfectly we might comply and fit into a particular role, after a while something will go wrong. When this happens it is actually a blessing. In Christianity suffering is seen as the way of the cross because through suffering we can awaken from our roles; to identify with them further becomes too painful. When the world takes away any comfort from you, use it as your way of finding the greatest comfort – your ultimate self.

How can we not be in constant stress and turmoil when we belittle ourselves so much? The unconscious ego is extremely negative and self-destructive. How indicative is it that a word like self-destructive exists in our vocabulary? We have seen the harm we are doing to ourselves every day. Why would we choose a life of such limitation and dread? Why do we believe we are inherently bad when in fact, the truth is the opposite?

This burden wasn't a conscious choice. But now consciousness is evolving through you. Until you awaken there will be specific lessons sent your way, over and over, until you finally learn them. It was always you who had to change, not the situation or the other person. Once you grasp this fact, you will free yourself from past karma. All lessons and troubles come your way so that you can awaken from your roles and chose the truth. Once you've grasped it, you'll no longer wish to cling to the smallness of the past. You'll forgive yourself and you'll return to the only thing that was ever real.

Buddha pointed to all of this when he spoke of the illusion of the separate self. You inhabit a body, a form, but you are not this form. Even Jesus pointed to the kingdom of heaven within. People have heard this statement many times but have failed to apply it. Instead, we decided to keep our ordinary ways and views. We gave up our tremendous potential and decided to worship things outside ourselves. We forgot that we are seeds, and that within us are states which are far beyond our current manifestations. It would be inadequate for us not to take this divine potential within ourselves into account. Religion is meant to be our soil for transformation; the ground cultivated for producing our highest self and providing the best opportunity for growth and development.

When you look within, the answer to everything becomes oneness and detachment from complete identification with form. Be alert, instead of being unconsciously run by the mind. It will continue to impose roles and conditions upon you. But just for a day, can you watch and see what happens when you don't believe everything the mind tells you? It might start out by telling you something negative, and then it will say something positive, but watch both thoughts with detached awareness. Then you can begin to realize that there are two in you. There is the *higher self* and there is another person, the *lower self,* or what can also be referred to as our mechanical nature, which you must fight. This is why the Bhagavad Gita describes the body as a battlefield.

Most people live their lives in a reactive state – meaning purely mechanical. They react to the thoughts in their mind and to the unconscious behavior of others without any filtering mechanism. This causes them to take things very personally and further strengthens the ego which leads to more illusion.

Religion can serve as your filtering mechanism because it allows you to correctly perceive the higher truth in any situation and stops the mechanical cycle of unconsciousness. Before a reaction comes up, be alert and watch it. Observe the body that you inhabit. Everything that it labels as real is only a small perception of reality. It is a distortion that is far removed from the truth. First, your brain has to recognize something. Then, based upon your past experiences, it will label it. This chaos is what we presently call our thoughts. We think that this unconsciousness somehow belongs to us, freshly originates in us, and we feel responsible for it. But if the definition of a thought is something that expresses your desires freely, then what we currently call "thinking" is actually far from that. Our current thinking can correctly be labeled as mental pre-programmed conditioning.

But the mechanical madness won't stop there. Based upon these labels (which happened unconsciously many years ago) we will experience yet another stimulus of either happiness or pain. Then, this final emotional stimulus will force us into action which our minds have labeled as being appropriate, even if it isn't, and the cycle begins all over again. This is why most of us are not truly awake. We have things happening unconsciously within us and we unknowingly identify with every label, every fleeting impulse, and these impulses create and control our lives. This chaos prevents us from connecting to our higher nature.

My only goal is personal transformation. What if everyone accepted this as their number-one responsibility? Not only would we stop completely identifying with and labeling form, but we would allow ourselves to open up and stop placing so much blame on other people. All responsibility would rest on us and our own transformation, because we would realize that once we change, everything else will change for us. This would also bring a humble attitude, love, and openness.

People like to work with other learners who are coachable, meaning they are open to bettering themselves. Have this type of relationship with yourself. Be coachable; be open to receiving guidance from your higher self. It is within and can be found when you silence your mental noise and place attention in the present. Eventually these coaching sessions with your higher self will become longer and longer until finally, you will merge.

We are all connected and when we choose to better ourselves we make the world a better place. We get what we give, always. When we give love to the world, it gives love back. This personal change, or shift in perception, or awakening, will happen once we've had enough of the old, and we are almost there now. Everything we see is a misperception. We think the body is real and the spirit is an illusion, when in fact it is the other way around. Human beings are part physical and part spirit. We are made up of atoms which are 99.999% empty space, and yet, we are fully focused on the limited material existence which is less than 1% of who we are. While on Earth, we must remain balanced in order to properly be both. Let's treasure both parts with loving-kindness and fulfill our purpose here.

Love is the purpose of all relationships. When we look around at most of our relationships we can easily see how wrong we've been about everything. When we don't fulfill our basic function, meaning our purpose of unconditional love, we suffer. Deep down we know this but instead of embracing it and freeing ourselves, we choose to live in illusion and create more suffering. In our current understanding of love, Plato was right in saying that love is a serious mental disease. We don't really know what it means to love.

We must think that unhappiness is serving some purpose. We unconsciously believe that enough unhappiness will get us what we want. A child will cry at the top of his lungs when he wants something and as adults we still revert to this method. However we know that when we give negativity, we receive negativity. A choice to remember this truth can only come from the higher self. We've built the life of stress up to such great heights that even a moment of happiness is a luxury we cannot accept.

But it's not about luxury. Happiness is about unlearning the false. Think of the person giving you the most grief right now. Now, say I *love you just the way you are*. Or maybe when you see him or her you can ask, *May I ask how you're feeling*? If you can say this out loud to the person then your natural state of happiness can emerge. If not, try saying it to yourself when you notice anxious thoughts clouding your mind. Allow love to enter your life. If you feel you can't do this, just try to recognize the resistance within you. Allow that resistance to be. Notice how your body and mind want to hold on to the negativity. Unconsciously, with every thought and action, you are either creating happiness or negativity for yourself. Even if you are "right", it's only a mental position; remember what is important to you - happiness. The other person was just acting in the only way his mind knew how, and it's not his fault he is unconscious with faulty mental programming. We are all like this until we awaken. Forgive him, send him love. In this way you are able to heal you both and enter the kingdom of heaven.

Happiness usually finds another major block in our work. Most of our work is based on the struggle to succeed. We give struggle and we create further struggle. Real progress would be occurring if things got easier after all this time. However, all we've managed to do is to complicate things further because we are thinking with limited minds. We keep filling ourselves up with endless data, the storage of which takes up most of our energy and prevents us from experiencing the states of unlimited happiness and success which are incompatible with limited perceptions.

When we place 'attention' on illusions, it cannot correctly be called attention. The real word for that is blindness. We are asleep. We are currently living with very little real attention, but such a realization is the first step in acquiring it, awakening, and leaving the dark. Paying close attention is one of the main teachings of Zen Buddhism. When we watch and pay attention, we begin to use self-observation as a means of awakening. Our attention is like a ray of light and if we shine it on the processes by which we live, our lives will begin to change and mirror this light. This is how we change our lives for the better, by observing, paying attention. Illusion can take place only when we are asleep. The slightest bit of attention can cast a ray of light on that which has thus far lived unconsciously. This light will make living in darkness impossible.

If we are truly serious about our human development, we must begin by placing our attention within instead of fully on the outside world. This is what true evolution is. Our illusions blind us by making us dependent on the outside world. Evolution and enlightenment are freedom from such influences. We are capable of reaching this kind of development, in which a true transformation will take place within us. This is what human evolution is – liberation from outside forces.

True freedom comes from fearlessly stepping away from the false self with all of its beliefs, associations, and handicaps. When we start watching our actions and our inner resistance, both at work and in our relationships, we will be one step closer to awakening. If such work is rightly conducted, we can take our ordinary states, our unconsciously mechanical and limited natures, and learn how to live again. We can receive a whole new mind, or rather, learn how to accurately use our current mind for the first time. We will leave the small parts of ourselves behind. We will manifest our highest possibilities and our deepest power. We will return to the real.

So if at work and in your relationships you become the quiet watcher, how will anything get done? When we hear things like "listen to your intuition" what does that mean? Does the soul already know everything? Your intuition has chosen everything around you so that you may evolve consciously. Everything is part of the path, part of dharma or the cosmic order. Embrace it. Place your attention in the present moment so that you can listen to your intuition and connect with your purpose. Then the doing will flow through you effortlessly. This is radically different from the distorted action we're used to taking.

There are some schools of thought that suggest you've chosen everything that is in your life, even the "bad". A better way to put this is that you unconsciously allowed it, because no one would knowingly desire suffering and unhappiness. We are all making choices that we think will bring us happiness. We've been living this way because we've been asleep and we thought that the ego was helping us and was actually who we are. However, within every struggle there is a dormant seed of opportunity. We can choose to awaken and in this way our struggles can turn into our blessings. Our freedom will come when we no longer label events in our life as good or bad, because ultimately they are all just situations which were designed to get us to awaken and they can take many different and fleeting forms which no longer have the power to devastate us.

When you're awake, which is the only time in your life you can freely choose your actions, your life will be different. How can it not be? You're no longer actively contributing to the delusion of the world. You have realized that you're here to experience it all, to let life flow freely through you, and you gladly pick the unlimited response to every moment.

Initially this can be hard to do because the ego is smart and it will continue to try and domesticate your mind. When you stop listening to the mind, life is filled with the *unknown*. Who are you now? This can be frightening and many people will turn away. As Jesus said, many are called but few are chosen. It takes a lot of courage to let go of the ego and to fit the unlimited inside of the small bodily container. You've listened to it for so long and unconsciously you've held the belief that it was here for your survival and to make you happy. When in reality, its survival and your happiness are incompatible. How much advice has the world given you about what happiness is? And who lives in this world? Considering the fact that most of the population is largely unconscious, this advice was given to you by an unqualified ego identity. You were given advice about happiness by the very vehicle which has thus far been used to prevent it.

Lesson 7: Today you are free to have loving relationships and to do work that brings you happiness. You are free to live abundantly because that is your only purpose. Nothing else is real to you anymore and you gladly watch life unfold all around you in the most wonderful ways. Letting go of the ego is allowing the inherent happiness that is within you to emerge. You are happiness and every moment of your life will reflect this.

CHAPTER 8

Birth, Death, and Awakening

Give birth to the true self and death to the ego, the life of illusion, so that your higher nature can emerge. But before that, an awakening is necessary, and another word for this is presence, because you are watching with alert, detached awareness. Presence forces you to go deeper within, and in this way, a detached watchfulness of everything in your life can be your best spiritual tool.

You are the light of the world and that is your only purpose. Realizing you are this light doesn't require the use of your mind. If it was something that you had to understand and to learn, then people would have been smart enough to have understood it by now. Rather, it is a letting go. Many of the thoughts going through your mind can be said to be repetitive and negative – they cannot be the truth when the most enlightened people to have ever walked the Earth have told us that love and light are the truth. And they've also told you to stop listening to your thoughts. The basis of life is love and cooperation. Competition at the level which we are presently experiencing is extremely destructive. You are here to let go, to realize who you are, so that you can transcend it all.

There is only one main teaching. There are no questions to ponder, mantras to chant, or scriptures to believe in. It is a realization of who you are once you drop identification with body and thought. It is who you were before you came here, and who you will be when you leave. To recognize this as your true identity while you're here is enlightenment. Then go on and live. Do as you will. After you achieve your primary purpose nothing else really matters. You respond to life as it comes and it lives through you. It is a most wonderful gift to observe and to give without clinging and attachment. But it's not an idea. It's a gift for the brave. It is a gift because it doesn't come from you – but from a surrender of you. As Zen master Dogen said almost one thousand years ago, "Birth is just like riding in a boat. You raise the sails and row with the oar. You ride in the boat and your riding makes the boat what it is."

Enlightenment is not about intellectual understanding. Throw that out the window. You know you're on the right path when you have no old beliefs to cling to and no new ones to find comfort in. All beliefs are gone and you are free, you are comfortable with the *unknown*.

Suffering is continuing to listen to the insane voice inside your mind. It can be likened to being another entity, a body of pain, which takes you over and lives inside you, controlling all of your actions and forcing you to unconsciously identify with it. This is the parasite that inhabits your body. This is the separation because you accept the biblical portrayal of guilt and punishment. All of this is pointing to the same truth. This thing that takes you over, whether you choose to see it as an energy field or a disease, forces you to believe it is you. It is composed of both your own pain and the collective pain of the human race, and all day long it tells you lies, it labels things and it punishes you. You believe these lies, and thus live in continuous conflict. This is the death that we are referring to – the death of this false entity which domesticates and regulates you, followed by the rebirth of your true self.

This is why the answer is found in the present moment - because it gives you the necessary space to watch this thing. The very fact that you can watch it means it's not really you. To be able to watch anything there must be an observer and something to be observed. This crucial space can also be created through meditation or reading spiritual books or going through a near death experience, among many other things. It doesn't matter how you create this space, what matters is that you have it. When you can silence your mind, the ego parasite, or just watch it while being fully alert, you can finally hear clearly what it's telling you. The next step is to stop believing its lies. What are its lies? Any thought that isn't love. God created you in the image of Himself, which means that you are perfect right now. There's nothing you can do to add or take away from the truth because even the best scientists alive today have no idea how to create something as perfect and complex as a human, or even something as "simple" as a living leaf. The little human eye is made up of over 1 billion parts, and a rocket, which is arguably our most complex invention, is only made up of 5 million parts. We cannot even come close to the mind of nature, let alone to comprehend her mysteries, because we are made up of the unknown which cannot be explored rationally. What we can see and study intellectually are insignificant details which fail to explain the real mechanism.

The truth will always be and it is not up to you. You can choose to temporarily not believe it while you search for other "truths" in the world concerning right and wrong, justice, and whatever other form it may appear to come in. Peace is the only truth and it can only be found in the present moment. Simplify! Let go of the details. Eventually the false will begin to lose its power and fall away because in the light only the truth can remain.

But you might think you still need this parasite inside of you to survive. How will you know what's right and wrong, or good and bad? In Buddhism, there are countless stories that depict the wisdom of not judging any situation. Because in the grand scheme of things, we have no idea if it's good or bad, and not only that, but even if it is good or bad it doesn't really matter because it's not permanent. It will come and go. It can only be good or bad based on the mental frame we see it in and this frame changes constantly. You might win the lottery but in a few years you might be bankrupt. Was that good or bad? You might lose your job and through that a door will open and you'll end up at your dream job. Was that good or bad? Paradoxically, failure can give birth to great victories. The general rule is to allow all experiences to come and go. Life is so complex, so perfect, that to try to label it or judge it with the very limited mind is impossible. There is no way that you or anyone else can possibly understand it. Perfect action will come through you when you are thinking with a silent mind – when it is not really you who is doing the action and when it isn't your thoughts that you are acting out. The best, wisest thing we can do is to surrender. To enjoy whatever comes our way in the present moment. This is salvation. This is what Jesus was pointing to when he told us not to cling to the world. Remember who you are, you are perfect, right now. Even the most successful among us, upon a closer examination, live very stressful and unhappy lives because their intellect can only take them so far. It can allow them to study the details but it can never allow them to know the ultimate truth because the truth would burn the intellect which tries to contain it. The mystery of life cannot be simplified into something soluble, which is good news because we can allow our minds to rest. We can relax and enjoy and allow life to be as it is, without our personal and often crazy opinions of how it should be.

Life is so good. Nothing else is real and we can joyfully release it. What a beautiful gift of transformation. Our purpose here is to love so that we can transcend. Use the Earth as your school for evolution. What awaits you after death is magnificent but what is even more magnificent is to realize this truth now and let it come through you into this world. Then you will achieve something that is even better than any astral existence – you will be united with consciousness.

When you celebrate your next birthday take the day to think about your journey here thus far. Do you really believe that the day you were born, however long ago, was the moment you came into existence? Do you really believe there was ever a time when you didn't exist? That cannot be. Everyone is part of the one life, part of God. We are all made of the same empty space which has no beginning and no end.

Many ancient cultures used to mourn birth because they saw birth as the beginning of limitation and illusion. For a few years after our birth, before the parasite or pain body can function in our minds, we are still connected to the source. As children our minds aren't developed enough to be able to identify and listen to discouraging messages, so we are free to enjoy ourselves. We must strive to return to our perfect state, return to the source, before we die. Our time here is so brief and fragile, subject to a million fleeting conditions. Stop trying to fight death and other conditions as if they were something that wasn't supposed to happen to you. Embrace them and allow them to show you your permanent identity so that all fear can be gone.

Nothing that happens here is really that important because what is true is true, it cannot be created or destroyed. The radio waves were there before we invented the radio, we just couldn't see them and didn't know how to use them. It's the same with the empty energy space within us. We have so much energy, we have simply forgotten how to harness it. Also, like all other electromagnetic waves, radio waves travel at the speed of light. To give you an idea of how fast this is, at the speed of light, a beam of light could go around the Earth at the equator more than 7 times in a second. Imagine how much energy that must take, and how much energy and pure potential the seemingly empty and invisible space around us contains.

These rays are constantly moving, just like the space within us. In order to receive radio waves, we must have a radio antenna. In order to vibrate with the highest frequency within us, we must have a way to silence ourselves and travel within. We're so attached to the outer layer of things. True creation cannot be seen, it is in the un-manifest, the side of the world which we label here as being non-existent. The side that always was and always will be has been temporarily obscured by a misguided belief system which we celebrate as our own separate sense of identity. But we came from the unknown, along with everything else here, and we can only see a tiny fraction of the truth with our human eyes.

When you make the present moment your only goal, you are promoting awakening in yourself and in the world. The empty space that fills us all is in constant communication with all. Be one with life, and let God's inspired thoughts be fulfilled through you so that all who come in contact with you can know the truth and the abundance and the peace which is within them as well. This space, this intense emptiness within you, is not of you. You cannot personalize it and you cannot enter it with a preexisting sense of identity.

God's creations cannot suffer. The only part of you that is suffering now is your false identity. There is a part within you which has never been involved with any of the misperceptions. There is nothing you have to struggle to create, and remember that as long as you are not connected to the depth of your true self, your presence, your being, you're not really creating. A Course in Miracles teaches that it is only what the go introduces that tires you. You're projecting and interpreting and shuffling around useless but temporarily visible objects. God created this experience for you and he will continue to create through you whether you are aware of it or not. If you remain unaware, you will remain in conflict.

Let go of your thoughts and choose peace. However, you may not be ready to accept peace. You may still believe that you are not perfect, not worthy, and that there is something you have to achieve on Earth to permanently add to your sense of self. Whenever there is such doubt, know that you have placed your trust in the part of you that isn't real. You are listening to the pain body, the parasite. Remember only peace is real because you were created in the image and likeness of God. Surrender your problems, and then watch the miracles take place in your life. This is the biggest gift. You will no longer be attached to the parasite. You'll be spontaneous, vast, and light. You'll remember who you are.

Do not deny the source of your creation and all your problems will be solved. Do you think the source of your creation is your mother or father? That they consciously created you and put you here? Most likely your mother and father are still spiritually unconscious and have no idea what you even like or dislike, let alone know anything about what it takes to create your existence. You ought to deny this belief in the corporeality of birth and death and everything that goes along with it.

If you really want a problem solved, you cannot doubt. To doubt is to cling to the identity of the little me. Do you want healing? Are you ready to let go? If we focus on perfecting within, we will achieve perfection in the outside world.

We've been taught to work hard and figure it out on our own. We were never taught that what we would figure out would turn out to be mostly wrong. We were never taught to surrender and to let go. Instead, we were taught to cling, to compete, to fight, to always be on the go. There are people who walk around with something or someone constantly talking to them in their ear. In the car it is music or the radio, at home it is television, up to the moment of sleep; at which point the restless thoughts in the mind take over. This is our life. This is what we fight so hard to protect. We have confused our insanity for wisdom and our destruction for progress. We think that from all this useless thinking and activity something intelligent will happen.

However we must think that the voice in our head is giving us a particular advantage, otherwise we wouldn't listen to it. If there is hell, or evil, it is not found in outside things such as poverty, war, or disease. It is within our own minds. It is listening to false concepts, believing in them, and then unconsciously acting them out. And the solution is so simple, so clear. Just stop believing what your mind tells you. Let the real mind, the knowing inside you, replace it.

How many times have you thought so hard and finally made the "right" decision and it turned out to be completely wrong? How many times have you taken something personally when you misunderstood someone who wasn't trying to hurt you intentionally? You don't have to live like this. You can be light and empty and wonderful. Embrace the emptiness; stop trying to fill your mind and your life with the destructiveness of the ego. Can you be still and enjoy peace? Does that sound unachievable? Stop creating unnecessary achievement. Know that there is already a force at work, an intelligence that is much more powerful than anything that you can ever hope to create with your judgements and opinions. This intelligence wants to express itself through you so that your experience can be what it was meant to be – heavenly.

Heaven isn't somewhere we go when we die; it is something that can be brought here now. You don't have to say you love or appreciate it because *it is* love and appreciation. *It is* joy. But this intelligence can only be heard in silence, stillness, and detachment. Just like the heavens above, you must become vast and empty and soar above the details of this Earth. This perfect program can only be carried out once you've wiped out your faulty processing system and viruses. Trust in God. He is within you and all around you, in all things, and all is well. You have the very best inside you but because of all the guilt, you believe you don't deserve it and every day you work very hard to obscure your own goodness.

We believe in the problems we unconsciously create so all day long we have something to do – we busy ourselves with the hard work of solving them, and then we create some more. During all of this busy activity we don't realize that we didn't need to do any of this to create a sense of worth. All it takes is a change of perception, which is already evident when you watch two people react to an identical event in different ways. The truly intelligent person is able to realize that there are no real problems that the small self can fix. A problem would mean there is something wrong with the actual design. The only problem is the limited perception of the unlimited design. You are a child, perfect, and God wants to create through you. He needs your voice in order to be heard and to have presence here. He will fix everything, instantly, because He will set you free. This is the miracle – a simple change in perception. Such a change can be your greatest weapon against illusion because it is unalterable, it opens you up to receive a higher power, and this opening never closes. You may call upon it at any time. The only problem is that we don't know this option is available because we trust the current world to provide the best for us; we don't realize that all it wants to do is to blind our perceptions and put us to sleep for as long as possible. The powers of the human consciousness are so vast, so great, that once we correct our perceptions it is unimaginable to think of the heights that the human race will achieve.

How do we solve big problems in the world? By realizing they're a manifestation of our unconscious misperceptions. We heal them by healing ourselves. Awaken to the truth and effective action will come through you. The world will joyfully mirror your identity, and as Lao Tzu said, you will, "Yield to overcome." Release and don't fight for or against anything. Become one with the world around you. Cease being fully attached and realize that everything in this world will pass away because none of it has a permanent identity. This includes family, job, body, beliefs, and relationships. Of course they are real, but you must realize that they are meant to be enjoyed and loved; they are the details, not the big picture, and they were never meant to cause you suffering. Don't fight in the service of anything other than heaven on earth.

You are not of this world and when you release your attachment to it you can walk through it freely, smiling and enjoying it, and why not? It's all temporary. None of it is the ultimate reality. But don't worry, you won't disappear into nothingness. Of course this physical world is real and it will continue to go on. But now it will be in a light and abundant way because things will flow as smoothly as they were intended to without anything from your little personality to add to it. You can live in the material reality, which is less than 0.001% of existence, but you can be centered in the deep space within you which is pure energy, and which makes up 99.999% of you.

Remember that only your little self needs thinking to survive – your higher self emerges without it. Your little person never needed to create anything. It needed to surrender to God and to enjoy itself in every moment. That's the truth and we've completely confused it. Instead we believe that we must rely on the little person and no matter how hard this poor little person works to understand and to do things there will always be suffering and difficulty. Maybe a brief moment of peace will eventually be given the little guy, but statistically speaking, it is unlikely.

The truth is that you deserve happiness and there is no part of you in reality that is that small. You were given this experience to enjoy and to be happy. God wants you to be happy and the entire universe will rejoice when you remember your true purpose. Everything up to this point in your life happened just as it needed to. How could it have been any different? It's gotten you here, which is good. People will try to pull you into their problems, their drama, because unconsciously they need your energy to keep their lives going. This is their food and their poison. Just let them be. Watch and enjoy. Drink your coffee if you wish, go to your job, and surrender as much as possible. The true sage continues to live in this world, because he or she wishes to embrace and overcome, not to escape, the human condition and everything that goes along with it.

You don't have to retreat to the mountains – *all you have to do is to watch your thinking*. Don't go below thinking, rise above it. Watch everything in the now. Make everything a part of your spiritual practice. Everything was placed here for your enjoyment – the beasts, the trees, everything. In the purely biblical sense, we are the kings and queens of the world already, everything is perfect and all we need to do is to correct our perceptions. In our perfect state we used to live peacefully with the animals, we never thought of killing them because we were already surrounded by abundant and nutritious food. We never struggled to survive; in the higher state such a notion of insufficiency is inconceivable. It wasn't until our recent human history that we fell under the grip of the ego. A long time ago we lived and created naturally and abundantly. We couldn't even dream of creating something as useless and unpractical as our present economy. This is our return toward that truth.

Lesson 8: Today, declare that you are spiritual. Take an oath of spiritual identity and realize the truth in every moment of your life. Step by step, your presence will transform the entire world.

CHAPTER 9

Evolution of Humanity

If you want the truth you can start by taking everything you think to be true and reversing it, or better yet, getting rid of it entirely. You think things happen to you, when in fact you have unconsciously chosen them. This life is beautiful and precious and in it you have the free will to choose whatever you wish.

The body tells us what to do and we obey, but it wasn't always like this. We used to build our own dwellings and grow our own food. The concept of land ownership was inconceivable and only applied in the most practical sense: if your dwelling was there, then it was yours. Our children lived near and with us and would inherit these properties. We loved ourselves and our world and disease didn't threaten us. We not only lived on the land but we felt that it was ours. We were an intrinsic part of the life around us and our homes were full of love because they were based on the truthful exchange of the things that really matter in life. We ate organic food and we were healthy. But then something happened and we fell asleep. We were lured into the idea of working for money, for paper, and using this to buy the things that we need. When we want an apple we can't go out and pick it, we must work for the money we need in order to buy it from the people that shipped it and did a million other unproductive things. Modern medicine isn't working because more and more people are becoming sick, and every other part of our economy mirrors our current unconsciousness.

The body is the unconscious state that most people inhabit and it is a direct reflection of our world. We were placed into these bodies, and we treat ourselves as slaves. How can inner liberation even be mentioned in such a state? We are almost proud of our mechanical living, our self-imposed domestication, and every day we are moving further away from true independence due to the lure of false luxuries.

Most people live their entire lives within a frame. They are shaped by other people's opinions and beliefs as well as their own delusions and limitations. Rumi wrote, "Your listeners love difficulties, not unity! Talk about world troubles. Don't distribute water from the fountain. They don't want that. In fact, they've loaded themselves with dirt to clog up the fountain. They'd like to shut it off!" The human race has learned how to domesticate itself down to a level so dull that the only gift that comes from it is an ever elusive sense of being "safe". We must surrender to the mystery of life. We can blame outside events, but in truth we must blame ourselves for believing in these roles and living up to them.

Life is full of conditions and it is the free flow, the trust, the allowing of these conditions to be as they are that brings us peace and liberation. When we do this, we are no longer living in the past or the future. Real change comes from within and it is a step that we must take. Don't try to resist anything in the outer world. This truth calls for a giant step into the unknown. At first, even being there for a moment is frightening. When we stop believing everything our minds and bodies tell us, we will be left in a space of disconcerting aliveness and self-reliance. Let me warn you now that initially it might not be comfortable.

Even though you are leaving the false and going toward the truth, your mind might convince you that you are doing something wrong and possibly suicidal. Just watch your thoughts and let them naturally become less real to you. If you fully let go of the old, recycled thoughts, who will you be? You will know nothing. You will be empty. And finally, you will be free and fully conscious for the first time in your life. A knowingness will arise in you, which will paradoxically allow you to admit that you know nothing. You will be connected to spirit, just like a child, and you will keep your highly developed human functioning. You will use it, and your brain, when you need to. It will no longer use you or trick you into identifying with it. You will be an adult who is connected to the source and you will be happy to experience whatever comes your way. There is only one consciousness, the space of pure energy, and you will finally be able to see it in everything. "Out of one, ten thousand things." It has created the myriad of things around you. You can continue to enjoy the things it has created, while remembering it for the first time, and consciously experiencing both the creation and the Creator.

Every religion points to the same truth. We can achieve our highest potential, our divine plan, and live up to the very best that is within us. We might stray and we might resist, or turn around, but we are always on the path. There is nothing else and nowhere else to go. Buddhism describes this path as surrender, as well as Christianity when it refers to suffering and the way of the cross. You are most likely reading this book because you have gone through some difficulties in your life, and now these difficulties can be transformed into a great gift, because to awaken spiritually is the primary goal of existence. The Tao Master Lao Tzu taught that difficulties are the very road to immortality. If we are able to meet them calmly and openly, everything we need to learn in order to develop ourselves will be revealed to us.

Yes, you can change your life if you change your thinking – but what's best is if you can take it one step further and become light and spontaneous because you are no longer attached to your life or to your thinking. This is what this book is intended for: to create a lighter mind within you. Your mind will become as vast as the ocean, instead of a small pond. "Do you know how many blessings you'll be able to receive then?" You can still enjoy life and your mental activity, but you know that none of it is permanent or could possibly add to the reality of who you already are. Every experience will delight you because you will be there to fully experience it. It's a very radical thing to suggest that as an adult, your chief aim should be to unlearn everything that you have learned up to this point. But the truth is just that simple and just that easily overlooked. We pride ourselves on our complexity, and when

Buddhism, Hinduism, or Christianity tells us to let go and look within, it sounds too easy. The fact is that if we wanted real success, we would live differently in a world of happiness and ease, instead of increasing suffering and depression. The only identity that needs all of our current complexity is the ego. Complexity is brain food for the ego and it is our job to eat less of it so that eventually the ego will recede.

Do you know how much human destruction we can stop when we let go of our separate ideas? Over the years, our own complex ideas have led to many wars and have killed millions of people. Our enemies can be found both within and outside ourselves. Personal individual enemies, ideological opponents of our groups, controllers of material resources, and wars of aggression, are simply reflections of our own shadows and lower natures. What if we could all be content to just rest calmly in the peace of the infinite power within us, and transform the evil back into the light? The one life that we are includes everything, both good and bad. Could we let go of all the complexity and remember how to thrive?

Looking around, it appears that we have no immediate neighbors to emulate. We are living on a speck of dust surrounded by space in all directions. We are free to make life whatever we wish. No one handed us an instruction manual and told us that it had to be this way or else we would all be punished. So, left to our own devices, we collectively agreed on what a normal life should look like.

Jesus said that the truth is *inside* of us. Responding to a question from the Pharisees about when the Kingdom of God would come, Jesus said, "The coming of the Kingdom of God is not something that can be observed, nor will people say, 'Here it is,' or 'There it is,' because the Kingdom of God is in your midst."[1] What this means is that in order to enter the Kingdom of God, humans must experience a collective awakening. This awakening is the correction of our misperceptions, our faulty mental programing, and a return to the higher states of consciousness. The Gospels wrote about this thousands of years ago, that we must 'awaken', and 'sleep not'. This is also why the commonly used metaphor of the caterpillar becoming a butterfly is so poignant – because eventually the poor caterpillar awakens out of its own, self-made suffocation. And what is even more amazing is that this suffocation, this cocoon, was the most necessary part of its evolution.

But still most people look outside because to look within for even a minute is too painful. Additionally, many have missed the great truth that we must awaken. Just like the Bhagavad Gita, which is commonly referred to as the "Hindu Bible", the Christian Bible was meant to be a transformative text for the individual personal internal transformation. When Jesus lived, he preached that he was the Son of God, just as we all are. He didn't say he was special, in fact, he said that we will do even greater miracles once we too discover this truth within ourselves and let the Father work through us. The Bible is full of many examples of our upward and downward tendencies, and ways to free ourselves from our bad qualities. But it is not only our belief in these stories that will bring salvation, but most importantly, it is the transformative journey that we embark upon.

It is good to compare the major truths found in many different religions. All teachings are important because they are geared toward different temperaments and understandings, all of which are subject to words which can easily become misinterpreted over the years. For example, the tone of God as vengeful goes against everything that Jesus taught his disciples. The Old Testament is filled with the vengeance of God and the belief in the specialness of a certain group of God's chosen people, to the detriment of all other human beings. If we wish to seek the truth we must become open to a unified view of life, to be inclusive rather than exclusive, and to realize that we are all God's chosen people.

The given antidote is self-mastery through awakening. A calm and silent mind opens the gateway to truth because it is what comes closest to consciousness here on Earth, and it is within us now. We must remain calm, and remind ourselves that we are pilgrims traveling on the path. In the Bhagavad Gita, for the highest self to win the battle against delusion, he must surrender control to God.

Lesson 9: There are no conditions, no functions, and no prices to pay here. That is not what life is for, so stop living in your mind and punishing yourself. Life is here for us and all we must do is let go and embrace it so that we can move forward into our next stage of evolution. As Jesus prophesied, the meek shall inherit the earth, and you become meek by letting go, being empty and free, and living a simple life led by your heart.

CHAPTER 10

The Sacrifice of Self

"There was a time before we were born. If someone asks, this is where I'll be, where I'll be."

-Talking Heads, from the song "This Must Be the Place"

We must realize that we have nothing to lose. Not only because our current way of life is unproductive and isn't worth holding on to, but also because nothing that is truly real can be threatened and nothing that is unreal exists – which is one of the major lesson from a Course in Miracles. We must be like Buddha, and discover our own nothingness. We are part of the infinite energy which expresses itself in this world.

All perceptions are separated as good or bad, profit or loss, cooperation or competition. The world is made up of these subjective perceptions. One who is able to remain calm is considered a "flower among men" and is able to stay connected and solely identified with his eternal nature. He knows his body and mind aren't who he really is. He knows he has been here before, will leave, and possibly come back. He knows that wherever he is, that is where he is supposed to be, and he is able to live a simple and peaceful life.

This is the experience given to us and we must walk through this transitory world, unaffected by the billowing waves, forever rooted in the depth of who we are. The Bhagavad Gita, Chapter 2, states that the noblest man is one who is calm, not affected by good or bad, and only a man such as this is able to achieve ultimate liberation. It goes on to state that the indwelling soul within is completely limitless and indestructible, unlike the material flesh, and even if you cannot sacrifice the idea of the material flesh, take a look around and realize that what is born will die and will be reborn again, so why fight what is inevitable? Someone who believes in birth must likewise experience death, and someone who believes death must likewise experience birth.

The fight is within us. We are all life. Based on the human genome project we know that are all made with the same code. We understand the biochemical nature of life, once one allows for the appearance upon the Earth of the necessary chemical elements, but scientists don't know where these necessary chemical elements in themselves originated – who made them, who wrote the code, let alone how or why.

We have the same DNA and we are all part of the same human race. What the mind perceives to be clear cut, huge, all-encompassing differences are misperceptions based on unconscious notions and opinions. This mind creates a "real" world out of energy, atoms, and molecules. Remember that our visible world is less than 0.001% of our existence. The atoms which we are made of are 99.999% empty space! But this space isn't really empty, it's full of energy and potential. It is simultaneously empty and dense. It doesn't really matter what we call this empty space, as long as we realize that it is the energizing principle that creates life as we know it. It is indirect and apart from matter itself, meaning that what we can see with the naked eye is not it.

In the spiritual community, this empty dense energy space is commonly referred to as the ether. It brings everything into existence – life, spirit, ideas, action, love. We can't quantify what it is or explore where it comes from. This giant force is above, within, and around us. It occupies all space, it is emptiness, and its power knows no end. It is variable, changing shapes as quickly as an amoeba. It readily assumes different variations, characters, able to play many kinds of roles. It is even kind enough to share some of its creative powers with us, and at the same time, it is able to convince us that we are somehow separate from it and that we are stuck in these limited roles. It is the movie, the actor, the director, the set – we are simply the materialized shadows of it on the screen. It is the *doer*, the performer and creator of everything. We are simply the vessels which it uses to create life upon this earth.

Remember what the Bhagavad Gita states: the flesh is a garment and only the eternal formless is real. The fight is the inner battle between sleep and awakening, truth and illusion, good and bad. There is only one reality and we've all heard about what it is – limitless love. Our suffering comes from our inability to experience this emptiness, this pure energy potential within us. We know that it makes up 99.999% of who we are, and that it is unlimited, but still we choose to focus on the very tiny and limited material existence, struggling and fighting over everything.

We are living through what can be considered to be an experiment of the ego. We have free will and as long as we choose to be in charge, God will not be able to guide us and we will not be able to experience Him within us. The veil will be there, and we will focus on the limited, less than 0.001% of actual existence. But in the space of consciousness is our only joy and peace. It cannot be found anywhere else. This play of form is here for us to return to God. Our true self was never threatened and none of the misperceptions were ever real.

We focus on building our lives around the most fleeting things in the universe. Nothing that we see with the naked eye is permanent. We can only discover the truth in eternity, in the here and now, without separation. Begin by observing and questioning everything that the body tells you. This will open the doorway and show you that there is indeed a different entity alive within you. And if you are brave enough to align with it and to let go of the old, then all will be well. Even if you can't, all will still be well, but you won't be aware of it.

We must begin to question that which we presently label as being real, that which we have accepted as the truth. That's all there is to it. This opens the door to miracles, changes in perception, and ultimately to seeing the actual goodness of life. In this physical world of ours we like to have very concrete material signs. But the unknown doesn't work that way. We must surrender all labels, all ideas of good and bad, and all of our demands. Everything is simply an experience. If you believe in good luck and bad luck, then two different powers are real to you – you haven't realized that only one of them is real and it is everything. Karma is self-imprisonment. To know God is to transcend all karma, all imprisonment, lack, and limitation.

Often our belief in karma can hold us back. We think that we are destined to experience good karma or bad karma based on our actions because it's what we deserve. If we harbor a lot of guilt, we will sentence ourselves to bad karma. However, whatever actions we've taken prior to this point had been unconscious. They were done with a mind that didn't know any better. They weren't our fault because we were asleep, or spiritually unconscious. Once we awaken to the deeper reality of who we are, we bypass karma altogether. We tap into the 99.999% of pure, abundant potential! The outside world, with its good and bad, has no power over us. We are free to just *be*. We no longer focus on the less than 0.001% of existence, the speck of dust which is our material form. For the first time we can consciously choose our actions and this will create a new future for us. We will tell this energy field what we want, and it will tell us what it wants, and together, we will create a new way of life. We will be free to do as we wish, which will be the same as the wishes of the universe, instead of being misguided by our own compulsions. All compulsions and limitations abide in the less than 0.001% of existence. We never consciously wished to create them; they created through us while we slept.

Getting back to the separation concept from the beginning of this chapter and the two previous chapters, what this really means is that you have a choice. There are two in you – the ego/unconscious self, and the vastly higher self that is free of all limitations. Only one of them is real. Our mission is to heal the separation and return to oneness and the beautiful peace which is life in the present moment. Allow yourself to be sucked into this huge energy vacuum, the wordless infinite energy pool within. A lack of resources could not possibly exist in a space of such abundance. When the body and mind become silent you can experience it. The smallest cells within you hold all of the potential and all of the knowledge that you need. You are here to awaken and to let go of the concept struggle. You are here to realize that there is only one power and it is abundant and good.

If this energy field molded itself into your version of God and then came to you and said, *Hey, it's OK, I really don't mind what you did when you [insert regrettable situation here],* would you be able to enter the present moment then and stop pondering? It's just like when you pray you say, *Thy* kingdom come, *Thy* will be done. And thank goodness for that because now we can relax and let go, which is all God wanted us to do in the first place. We didn't need to think about or to solve our own problems. This is how ascension happens – through acceptance. Only the ego needs to analyze and separate. All of the greatest people have told us to surrender, but instead we gave ourselves the really tough job of trying to create our own solutions, struggling in the 0.001% material world with its limited resources, without realizing that we were always meant to receive.

In every moment our bodies are using up energy – we need food, we need sleep, and we if don't get it we die. We squeeze this energy from our daily life, but why can't we discover the energy within, and use it to replenish ourselves instead? When we tap into our infinite inner potential, we are able to consciously receive in every second of our lives. Such living creates true mastery. With this knowledge now freely available, we can stop placing our attention on the outside world and step inside for being. We can forgive ourselves for the past and let go of the future because we know that we cannot simultaneously cling to a mental position and be peacefully still. To connect with being, we must put down the mental position and the attachment to the outside world.

Lesson 10: Today you no longer see yourself as a victim and you show compassion toward the unconscious behavior of others because you know they have not yet seen the peace of God. And that's it. You've glimpsed awakening. Now, go on to repeat this throughout the day if you feel any frustration, negativity, or irritation. Know that negative emotions within you are just the lower self trying to run the show again. Remind the lower self of what you've learned today, and relax into the deeper peace of your higher nature. All is well.

CHAPTER 11

The Elements of Human Life

If you are still reading this book then you have silenced your mind and can agree that we've gotten it all wrong up to this point. People say to keep dreaming but also keep your day job. The truth is that your day job is a dream, maybe even a nightmare, and the inspired thing that you feel compelled to pursue is the truth that you should keep. Anytime there is effort or struggle, stop it. Life is at ease, so be at ease. When you're aligned with life, things flow smoothly because you are connected to infinite energy and potential. You are supposed to follow your dreams and flow smoothly with life because within them is your love and your purpose, which are one and the same.

What we see as normal life is actually somewhat unreasonable. As the western cowboys say, *Life is overly civilized, not enough frontier left*. What we deem as being civilized and as progress is actually a deadening, an untruth, and it is inorganic and responsible for much of the destruction which we label as progress. We can eat better, take better medicine, but the truth is that we must change the very structures responsible for regulating these behaviors within ourselves. We must change what we are hungry for and what we are willing to believe.

We read autobiographies about "successful" people and dedicate our lives to emulating them. But happiness cannot be found there, it can only be found within by following our own special path. We were made with happiness. We must be present enough to eliminate the noise so that we can forgive, heal, and be kind.

It's just like when you drive down the highway and see trash littering the roads. It's there until you pick it up and get rid of it. Over the years, chances are there has been a lot of trash that has accumulated in the inner roads of your brain. You see this trash and confusion everywhere you go and in everything you do. You cannot clean it up by examining it piece by piece with the rational mind because that would take an entire lifetime. That is problem solving with the brain because just like any muscle, it is limited by its linear rationality. You can only clean it all up instantly with the magic vacuum of your infinite energy and intelligence, by relaxing and letting your higher self take care of it. Only this inner vacuum has solution consciousness. You will not solve anything when you examine each piece of trash. Contrary to what many believe, you don't need to go over every life event and learn from it – you need to create a new mind within yourself. Divine guidance is within you and will tell you everything you need to know. What would have taken you a lifetime to accomplish comes instantly through God. The only thing you need to do in order to receive this gift is to surrender to the presence and guidance of your higher nature.

We not only have to deal with our own negativity, but also that of others. For someone who is unaware of the spiritual path, to give a heavy-handed response such as "it is all an illusion" is too much. It will only upset him further and he will be forced to work harder to find problems "out there" to complain to you about. Know that your presence in these situations, which means your connection to your higher self instead of the material world, is doing more than you realize. Even if the other person becomes upset or doesn't acknowledge it, you are planting the seed of awakening within him and simultaneously watering your own garden. Don't be afraid of being simple. Be afraid of confirming the false stories in others and contributing to them.

Many people experience trouble practicing present moment awareness because they are attached to roles supporting the family, such as being a mother or a father. A complete abandoning or detachment of thought seems very insensitive and disruptive since many mothers and fathers do not live for themselves but for their families. In this regard, the Bhagavad Gita is helpful and describes three basic levels of consciousness which are found within all humans: happiness, activity, and difficulty. Each of us is a mixture of the three, and finding the proper inner balance is ultimately what this inner work is about.

The ultimate level of consciousness is reached when you are able to be happy and free of thought in the present moment and you are simultaneously grateful for everything. This is where saints and enlightened people are found and this is our ultimate goal. The next level is action, which is sometimes good and at other times misguided. The ideal would be to bring a certain level of happiness and peace so that the action can be further directed upward toward spiritual pursuits. This is where a happy family would abide. The lowest level of consciousness can be described as laziness, inactivity, abuse, and problem-focus. All outer events are orchestrated to be in alignment with our current level of consciousness, because our level of consciousness creates our outer world. When we elevate our consciousness, we thereby elevate our world.

If you feel complete surrender is too much and may cause too much havoc for your family, then just take it a step at a time. Try to bring peace and happiness into your present actions. This is the ultimate goal; this is complete freedom from fear and full faith in God. This is where stepping into the unknown will ultimately lead you. This is the space of 99.999% pure energy, because you are no longer constrained by the material limitations of the mind. But you're probably not going to get there overnight, so take it a step at a time. You are stepping away from false comforts and into the unknown. It's not easy and it takes a lot of courage. Don't overwhelm yourself. Eventually, all of the restless activity can stop and you can realize that you are already free in yourself.

Our world is currently predominantly absorbed in the level of consciousness which is full of conflict, suffering, death, mental dullness, and helplessness. We even fight to protect ourselves from self-improvement. We become jealous or resentful of the peaceful and happy people around us, and we think it must be some kind of lie.

Perhaps this is why we turn away from self-mastery – our own current dominant level of consciousness despises the level of consciousness found above it. This is the natural resistance to change, and it will persist until life becomes so horrible that we wish to evolve no matter what the cost. Contrary to what we might believe, we don't like to evolve. We are forced into it.

Wherever you are now, realize where your next level of consciousness should be, and strive to get there. Then, everything will change. Once you begin moving up the scale, the forms and your relationship to them will change. The difficulties which you thought were impenetrable, the problems, the unanswered questions, will suddenly be solved or cease to bother you. They simply mirror the degree of consciousness which you currently possess, and your new degree of consciousness, your new mind, will shine a light on the dark and cause many of the past problems to disappear since they needed your lower level in order to survive.

See the qualities which the people in the next level of consciousness emulate, and let them come forth through you. Once you begin to act with a higher consciousness, you will attract better events and outer conditions. It is up to us, we choose which level of consciousness we wish to be at because all the levels are present within us in different amounts, and then our conciseness, our current mix, creates our outer world. The only thing we don't have control over is realizing the fact that we have control in the first place.

People who are living predominantly in one of the lower levels, dealing with helplessness and struggle, *don't realize they have a choice*. They accept the limitations in the 0.001% of existence because they think this is all there is. This realization of choice over your mental state is a mysterious gift. Somehow, openness for change comes. The Bhagavad Gita, Chapter 14, states that those established in the mode of goodness or happiness rise upward; those in the mode of passion and unfocused action remain in the middle regions; and those steeped in the lowest modes of illusion sink lower still.

When we reach the highest level of self-awareness, we live in a world of solution-consciousness. This is a world of possibilities because we live with the full realization that this is all a wonderful game. None of the outcomes are ultimately permanent; they will pass, no matter how good, and they are certainly not our ultimate identity.

In regard to the question of surrender and dealing with responsibility, this is what we're really talking about. There is a part within us that already has the solutions and wants to take action. The problem is that most of us are unaware of this part of our consciousness and we don't feel comfortable relying on it because it is unknown. Let's take a commonly known spiritual metaphor. Suppose you are a class of school kids. The class is either run by the lower levels and is in disarray and confusion (which is what happens when the teacher isn't present), or the class is more harmonious and organized (such as when the teacher is running the class). The teacher is your mental state, and ideally, we want the best version of it to be in charge. The children represent your primitive senses and emotions and fears, and in most, they are allowed full dominion and are running wild. This again points to why all of the teachers of the past have told us to awaken – awaken the schoolmaster (your higher nature) who is supposed to be in charge of the class, meaning the self.

We cannot deny that such a shift in perception might be a risk. But if we are sincere and dedicated in our search, we must be willing to go forth anyway. The more we risk, the more we will attain. Once you embark upon this path, and see the madness of the world, it will be almost impossible for you to resume your regular life. Many spiritual teachers refer to your old life as your "ordinary chair." A person who hasn't strived toward spiritual liberation is happy to sit in his ordinary chair and is presently enjoying life, because to him, it does not matter that he is limited. He is blissfully unaware. A person who is spiritually liberated is a thousand times happier, but, for the seeker caught in the middle without a chair since he has not yet reached ultimate liberation, he is the most miserable of all. In order to reach the ultimate liberation, or freedom from influences outside and inside of us, we must be willing to take the risk, and for a while, remain without a chair. This is the step into the unknown, the wilderness, the death of the small self, or the dark night of the soul.

There will come a time when you will no longer be trapped in misleading thoughts, but for the time being, simply try to watch as much as you are able, without becoming overly fearful. The Bible tells us, "In all your ways submit to Him, and He will make your paths straight."[1] Once we know the power of our thoughts, we will take powerful action and unseen forces will come to our aid to remold our bodies and our lives.

In times of suffering, remember that this is the world that was given us to live in, and our only task here is to purify ourselves. The Kingdom of Heaven is already here, we don't need to wait until we die. We can enter into a blissful oblivion of the world and men forever while at the same time retaining boundless pity and compassion. We can stop at the threshold of Nirvana, the ultimate pure state, and willingly continue to play roles here for the sake of others. Only now, the great delusion will be gone and all suffering will leave along with it.

We reach perfection by happily accepting everything around us. St. Therese of Lisieux urged us to strive toward perfection, because that is the way to achieve happiness. To her, being perfect was to fully surrender the small self and to follow the will of God. This is why Jesus said "be ye perfect, even as your Father in heaven is perfect." This perfection comes from surrendering our own thoughts and desires, and letting God guide us in all aspects of our lives; we must surrender our separate identities and the labels that go along with it, and "be in this world, but not of it." We become perfect not by working on our personalities, but by surrendering them entirely.

If you are drawn to this contemplative life, and if you are worried about what is to come, have faith. Know that there is a greater force in charge and all of your material needs will be met. You are wonderful, and your roles will flow flawlessly through you. Roles are a necessary part of human life here on Earth. You will still carry out these roles, but now there will no longer be suffering in it because when you know your true identity, nothing on Earth can sadden you.

We will no longer be only human flesh. We will stop cherishing our identifications. We will realize that our identifications actually prevent our freedom. They prevent us from achieving anything of actual value.

Lesson 11: Today, be ye perfect and make your mind clear and beautiful again. As you do this all of life will rejoice with you. You're here to save, and you will get what you give.

CHAPTER 12

The Impact of our Thoughts

"We speak wisdom among the perfect or initiated, not the wisdom of this world, nor of the rulers of this world, but divine wisdom in a mystery, which none of the rulers of this world knew."

-1 Corinthians 2.6-8

The documentary *Free the Mind,* released in 2012, directed and written by Phie Ambo, showed that we still have no idea how conscious experience arises from this blob of matter that weighs three pounds and is commonly referred to as a brain. We know that this brain changes throughout our lives, similar to the way our physical appearance does, but we have no idea how. Although we are made of 99.999% empty space, this brain somehow makes the 0.001% seem like the ultimate reality.

You can choose to change your brain for the better by being happier, kinder, and more compassionate. These are all outer things that happen once you connect with your inner purpose. Contrary to what many believe, when you become enlightened you can still function in the world. You don't just sit around or disappear into nothingness, at least most of us don't. You enjoy the world and you play a vital part in healing it. There is more here than what meets the eye and compassion can open up that higher dimension for you. This higher dimension isn't necessarily a healing one because it transcends the need for healing – it creates a new relationship between you and the world.

Ordinarily we have very little control over our minds, usually not enough to choose compassion before we automatically act out our emotional states with our limited mind frames. Imagine if we could stop, censor ourselves, and become kinder people. In school there should be a new major: mind sculptor. It only makes sense since we know that our minds create our reality. Remove components and unlearn. It's not about adding anything. It's about unknowing everything that was false. When a sculptor gets ready to sculpt, he chips away. He keeps chipping until he finally gets the result he wants: that sought-for image that was always there. We become perfect by removing components.

All we have to do is be open to the fact that there is a better way and that the world is broadly unconscious. Imagine how much more glorious the world will be once we awaken. Not so long ago, due to the lack of access to clean water, people went through their days drinking wine. They were partly drunk but they still managed to accomplish things. Well, we're not too far off from that state. The way our minds function unconsciously is very similar to a state of drunkenness. How else can you explain being unhappy and fighting with the people you love most in this world? It's madness. Examine yourself, *Know thyself,* learn who you are.

We have taken our existence for granted, and this has forced us to stop questioning our origins. We falsely believe that we know exactly who we are. We have forgotten that 'Know thyself' means to observe unconscious tendencies, which are largely the same in all of us. We think that we already do this, and that everything we think and do is up to us. We don't realize how mechanical and reflexive we are; that we are asleep and are shaped constantly by the outer world. This is why many don't even begin the search – because they mistakenly think that they already know who they are and what life is all about. They think that this material stuff is the truth, that it is all there is. It is our own fault that we not only fail to see the truth all around us, but that we don't even strive to do so.

If we remain unconscious, then we are not free either in our outer manifestations or in our inner lives. We are proud and this blinds us to our own faults: our lack of love and patience, our minor irritations with petty maters, our constant distractions. We are all perfect examples of mechanical existence. We take in food, produce energy, and then waste it ceaselessly in all our struggling. And out of this, we somehow feel we are free and in charge.

We know nothing about ourselves or about being human. We are fully focused on the physical, and unaware of the metaphysical, the pure energy with which we are made, and which holds all the solutions and power in the universe. We fell very far, and as long as we remain focused on the material level, we will continue to live in the illusion of lack. We have trained ourselves to forget exactly who it is that we are.

For example, our current state has brought us to a place where our medical system has turned into an income producing activity. More patients means more money. We spend the most money on health care compared to any other country, and yet America ranks pretty low in actual health measures worldwide. A high percentage of all doctor visits are due to stress. PTSD and veteran suicides are at an all-time high. Yet our military and defense industry continues to thrive and to recruit more soldiers to serve our ideological justification for our foreign military actions. We spend billions of dollars fighting wars on drugs, and this reckless attention on problems only creates more wars and more drugs to help us deal with our problems. All of this wasted effort and resources must be cleaned up through an inner purge before we can claim to make any real progress. The problem isn't in any outer event, but in our limited perception of these events.

The Bible states that the battle belongs to God, not man, and to "cast thy burden upon the Lord." When we do this, we are blessed with solution consciousness. In the Bhagavad Gita, God tells Arjuna (the higher self) that he can win only if he surrenders control to God. If we take this burden upon ourselves, we violate the law. We must give up our perceived control over our outer conditions. We must cast our burdens on the higher nature within, and go free. Then, miraculously we will see clearly. It is impossible to have clear vision while in the throes of problem-consciousness. We must stop filling our minds with fear and suffering and allowing our imaginations to take us to places that we never wanted to go, places of greed and lack. We must give up our fears in order to reach our happiness – we cannot keep both.

Remember that in the lower state, solution-consciousness is not possible because all attention is on the physical. It is written in Matthew 18:3 (NIV), "Truly I tell you, unless you change and become like little children, you will never enter the kingdom of heaven." Children are free to live in the space of pure energy. They haven't learned how to rely on themselves and live focused on doubt, lack, and physical limitations.

When we awake, the useless suffering will cease. This suffering exists only while we sleep. All that is needed to solve our problems is to awaken – to realize that we can stop all of this with a letting go, a surrender of the problems. This is hard when the entire world around us is propagated by these delusions and everything that we do on a daily basis only strengthens these illusions and makes them seem more real. We live in a world that is asleep, consciously speaking, and it is no small thing to begin to remember that we can wake up. To realize that we have a choice, to have the desire to awaken, to become perfect through surrendering, is a great deed in itself.

We must pay attention to the good and cease being blinded by our own illusions. But this is something that we have trouble remembering. We collectively suffer from amnesia. If we were still connected to the truth we would know that we are meant to be happy, robust, and full of life. Not to hunch over our desks all day and then continue to sit as we drive, followed by more sitting when we get home. We continue to stagnate ourselves and create false notions of progress. We can either choose to chip away at our health or we can improve it. It's a myth that our health gets worse with age. There are many cancer patients who have increased their health while still living with cancer. There are many 60-year-olds who are healthier than 30-year-olds. We are vast and mysterious, we are not stuck, we do not need to remain asleep.

Don't be afraid to be a pilgrim, go within, and question yourself and what you have come to believe. The truth is that the abundance of the world, with its infinite health and happiness, is already a reality within you which you never truly left. It wishes to shine through you and to come forth into this world once again.

You must choose how you see the world and hopefully you will do this consciously. God loves the world and to be enlightened is to be like God and to love the world just as it is in this moment. This is why you must be perfect to view the world as God does – to let go of preconceived notions and to accept it just the way it is. You cannot possibly love this world with your current perception of it, which is why you must surrender and unlearn. Nothing else is real. This is the world God loves, not some idealized version of it in the future that the weak little people of Earth have to struggle to create.

None of the problems we are trying so hard to fix on the outer level are ultimately real and they will all vanish once we let go of the roles, stories, and ideologies that these problems rely upon and learn how to harness the pure energy with which we were made. Every form, every experience, is God's dream. When you are fully absorbed in God's dream, you have no desire to focus on the problems, which is why they don't seem real to you anymore. You become focused on the fact that this is all oneness experiencing itself in different forms. This is a temporary manifestation, and in this way it can be compared to a dream. Knowing this comes from surrendering to the present moment and being aware of your inner state; watching everything with detached awareness, as a higher observer of the body, realizing there is another reality and order to things.

When you are no longer acting unconsciously you can monitor and become aware of every belief and choose whether or not you wish to act it out and bring in into this dimension. It was always already here and you simply decided to bring it to the visible world. It's no less real and it's not good or bad. It just is.

Why would you choose to believe in problems? Because they have given you an identity which you have worked your entire life to build and to maintain. When you surrender your own thoughts, the thoughts of God are able to enter, or rather, to be seen, because the fog has finally lifted. In order to hear them you must be still. How can you possibly see peace in this world, in our world, with a mind that has been conditioned to sustain conflict? Our perceptions of fear and suffering will be gone, and with them will come a change in our daily situations. But we must first develop the consciousness to understand who we really are and how life here works. Naturally, humanitarian tendencies will arise.

We must surrender our previously held conflicts and notions. Even those who fight for peace are really fighting for a particular story. We must become still, give up our armies, and focus on fixing our inner mental and emotional states. Then, the state of our outer world will fix itself in order to reflect our new sate of consciousness, because really, both the outer and inner worlds are just one state of consciousness, manifesting in many forms. Nothing is permanent; there is no real identity here on Earth for anything. No story remains true in the long run and we can let go of our entire life archives and save ourselves the headache of holding on.

We must evolve. The way we are living now will eventually disappear. After more people awaken to the truth there will be a radical shift in consciousness. Things will change and it will be heaven on earth, but it cannot be attained using the ego. Heaven will no longer be seen as the reward for a life of struggle. It will be seen as our birthright and a natural extension of our earthly existence. This shift isn't something we must concern ourselves with. It will happen of its own accord, at the right time.

The process of awakening and letting go of all pain can be hard at first. Most of us have been so tough on ourselves that we've found endless ways of punishment. Be kind to yourself and to those around you. Here you sit, reading about how in reality you are the light of the world. You might be intellectually in agreement but as soon as a separate thought enters your mind and you believe in it, everything you have read here will recede.

Your mind will suggest that you don't deserve to be the light of the world. That God must have been mistaken. That you weren't made in the likeness of God and that therefore you are entitled to some other truth which you can follow; some other price and punishment that you need to carry out because you are a separate person. That although this world is impermanent and although you formerly have been unconscious, somehow you must pay for all of the "mistakes" you've made because they were consequential. You believe your experience here has somehow altered the truth within you of who you are; that somehow this tiny planet, with its heavy and fleeting experiences, is the only thing that is real.

Through your unconsciousness you may continue to create situations which will reinforce your beliefs. Even though you have every intention to be happy and to stop suffering, somehow the voice in the head is still in control of you and you are subconsciously identifying with it. This can only happen when you don't watch and control your inner state. How will you know when you have stopped listening to the madness? You'll feel at peace, complete, and full of love. You'll remember that you are perfect no matter what has happened here, just like everyone else. You'll become light and spontaneous and kind and you'll find that for the first time you actually enjoy your life. You'll be living your purpose.

We have placed all of our faith in the scientific mindset and it has put us in a very tight corner. We used to proudly say, 'I'll believe it when I see it,' but such a line is no longer considered to be the height of wisdom. We realize that we are blind to the majority of the phenomena that surrounds us. We live in a world which, for the most part, we cannot see. But this doesn't mean that because we cannot see it, it is somehow just happening or is accidental. If science cannot go somewhere and prove something to our limited visible senses, it doesn't mean that it is not a part of life, or is not important to it. There are places where science simply cannot go, and it would be arrogant to say that such places are somehow less real.

If you stay diligent and watch the voice in your head with as much detachment as possible you'll realize that not everything this voice tells you is true. And that is so wonderful. Whose voice is that? That voice is the accumulation of all of the unconsciousness in the world and it is not who you are. Our minds and memories are all connected and this negative energy has a grip on all of us. As soon as you begin to question it, it will start to lose its momentum. Why? Because it was never real. It needed your unconscious identification with it in order to make it real. The truth doesn't need anyone to believe in it because it's the truth and it will be there no matter what. Gravity was around before anyone actually discovered it. Even when you were unconscious and didn't believe in love, it was still there, waiting for you to remember and come back. What a wonderful time we're living in now, when so many people are choosing to awaken once again and we can accelerate this process by dedicating every day to choosing the truth.

You'll find yourself sustaining moments of silence, peace, and happiness for longer and longer periods of time. Right action will happen through you, without any mental interference getting in the way. But wait, how can this be? Am I not the person who is thinking things and must continue to think things in order for the world to function? Or, am I something else? Is the world something else? Something deeper that isn't subject to labels and stories? Do I actually not need all of the mental activity that has been causing me such grief? All of the needless thinking when the world can and does flow perfectly without it? Thinking is wonderful but only when it is done in a constructive way and on your own terms.

You might look at yourself in the mirror and not be particularly happy with what you see. And yet, if you connect with the life and energy within, you can learn to laugh at yourself because anything you see in the outer world pales in comparison to what you've discovered within. You know that face isn't permanent, that it's just part of this current story. You awaken more and more and as the ego loses its control over you your life becomes filled with ease. As you look on things lightly, with forgiveness, the story with which you see things begins to change so that it perfectly reflects your inner state of wellness and light.

You are a magnet for all of the good things in this world. Happiness, health, and abundance are inherently designed to flow to you. It is your natural state to feel joyful and at ease. The alternative is the crazy story we've unconsciously decided to identify with because we tried to punish ourselves and the world. But remember that difficulties are here to accelerate your awakening process. The difficult scripts aren't true. You are a Son of God and you've returned to life, awakened from the dream of deadness and struggle. You've found your power. Why else would you be here and what better revelation could you ever hope to experience? You are no longer a stranger in a strange land because you now recognize yourself as part of life itself. Not removed, but connected to all that is. It all belongs to you, all the good in this world.

This is your only purpose. Nothing else is real. However, your mind will continue to make you believe in struggle and separation and some future-only salvation. If you feel like it's too painful to live in this world you might turn to drugs, or alcohol, or food, but that can all stop. If there is currently any suffering in your life - use it as your spiritual practice. Accept it and let it show you the truth. Let go, watch, and stop believing everything that goes through your mind. Remember that you are something much greater than the thoughts in your head.

You might have heard it said before that we are all actually spirits having an experience here on Earth as humans. We've become so identified with the story, with the human part, that we've forgotten about the spirit. However as we realize the madness of the ego, we'll be able to evolve. We'll return to our spiritual nature with a deeper sense of understanding that our brief foray into suffering has given us.

Instead of conflict, offer peace. Become easy-going. Say yes. It's amazing but you'll find your problems solving themselves in the most wonderful ways. This is what a miracle is – a change in consciousness followed by a corresponding change in the outer world. Miracles mean big changes and at first they might seem scary because sometimes they appear wrapped in circumstances which you might deem to be bad. You might lose a job or a relationship, but this change is your miracle if you allow it to be.

Material things are wonderful but when you know the real depth of who you are, they cease to be all consuming because they can't possibly add to the amazing identity that you already have. And it's not really an identity, because you are everything. How can you be just one little thing anymore with a preset expiration date? You are aware of life and you are the awakened part of it – you allow life to be.

Now let us be clear; when we say surrender, it doesn't mean that the mind, body, and emotions will automatically fall into a state of blissful peace. Most likely the body and emotions will be in a shockingly horrible state. It isn't easy, not even remotely. The voice in the head will make up many stories and judgements and the body will experience pain and discomfort to the point where you might think that your chest will explode from all the pressure. But as much as you can, let it all happen without attaching yourself to it and entering into the drama. They are just stories, after all. Try to watch as much as possible, as if you were watching a horrible movie. The realization that you are the one perceiving it all is the most important discovery you can ever make.

In a few minutes, hours, or days the voice of the ego and the corresponding pain will begin to subside. The new energy field of your body will make it hard for it to stay, but it will try to come back occasionally because your body is the only existence it can ever hope to have. This process in Christianity is referred to as the way of the cross, but not the Catholic liturgical practice called by the same name. What we are referring to is surrendering your suffering to God. Many religions believe that you cannot find God without suffering, without the pain that Jesus endured on the cross, and so if there is suffering in your life now you can choose to perceive it to mean that you are on the path to God.

God is trying to get your attention so that you can awaken. Just hold on and soon the pendulum will begin to swing the other way. There's no guilt, or worry, or doubt; you just watch with as much detached presence as possible. Wouldn't you rather allow perfect thoughts to filter through you, instead of the untamed, destructive, and primitive ones of the ego? Then, you will realize your spiritual reality. You will no longer see yourself as being merely the material body.

When you practice detached awareness you can experience yourself as not even being in a body. If you are solely identified with the body, then life is shallow. There is no space, depth, inspired thought, or perfect action. The body creates a life that is full of conformity and dullness. When you see yourself in this way, subject to your moods and emotions, believing they are the ultimate reality, you are seeing yourself as a body and you are unconscious. When you realize yourself as spirit, having a temporary body, being one with life, then you have made the ultimate realization and all of the suffering was worth it because it got you to wake up.

After the ultimate realization, you are limitless. This is what the Buddha was trying to get people to realize – he pointed to the fact that you need to surrender your sense of a separate self, of the little me, so that you can see the truth. Once the little me becomes too horrible and full of suffering, people are usually able to surrender it. Unfortunately there are other times when they can't, and the pain creates even more unpleasant stories to believe in.

In the end, pain will be whatever you allow it to be. Remember that it can transform you if you let it because only light is real and even pain is light in disguise. St Therese of Lisieux wrote about a dream she had as a girl, when she saw two little devils dancing. She said that as soon as she looked at them, they became irritated, frightened, and ran away. This is what the dark is – a coward that can only live when you don't notice it. Your attention will frighten it away because it cannot stand the light.

Emptiness focuses our attention on the light and dispels the darkness. It allows the universe and thoughts of God to fill us – instead of our old, limited thoughts and ways of living, which are unnoticed little devils. It is all just a change of mind. The brain, our instrument for life here on Earth, gets an upgrade, or maybe just a reboot, and returns to its original perfect state. From there it will reach new heights of consciousness. Rumi wrote, "To praise is to praise how one surrenders to the emptiness."

We have been placed in these bodies so that we may become like sponges, and allow Gods voice to speak through us to the world. Higher consciousness, or the Christ within us all, is here to help bring us into the next dimension.   All of the great masters have been saying the same thing in one way or another – stop thinking and surrender. When you begin this practice, you will quickly realize how little control you have over your life and how possessed you are by your imagined fears. Your liberation won't be easy, but it will certainly be worth it.

You don't have to keep thinking, censoring yourself with "good "thoughts. Emptiness is your flashlight and it will guide your way through the dark. When you watch the thoughts the false slips away and the real thoughts naturally emerge. They aren't really yours because these thoughts of truth are within us all and cannot be created or destroyed. There was nothing your body or your brain needed to add.

All that is presented in this book, you already knew, but had forgotten. It was always there, just like the fire in the match. The match does require to be struck by the hand of an external being, and metaphorically, this is your longing for higher consciousness. This longing is all that you need. Just like in *The Matrix*, Neo felt different and ready to awaken, and his desire led him to Morpheus, who unplugged him from his false self. The truth was always within you, waiting for the right conditions to emerge, to be ignited. You didn't create, you didn't destroy, you just shifted your perception of yourself.

Every moment of every day most people sacrifice both their peace and their freedom. And for what? In order to belong to a world that is unhinged. This sacrifice brings a never-ending search and a dissatisfied victim identity. We make up roles and assume these identities to be the absolute truth. Of course we are not these things, and in time, they will fall away. Yet most people still spend their entire lives clinging to their self-made illusions.

If you see the world in this way, then death exists for you and you have no idea who you really are. You have a purpose here but until you figure out what life is, you will remain blinded by struggle. The first step toward finding your purpose is to connect with your indwelling higher nature. This is what life put you here to do.

Why did Jesus speak of forgiveness? Why was it his main lesson? In

Buddhism they say that if you are angry for any reason you are automatically wrong. When you choose to deny another person the gift of your vision, your ability to see past his bodily form and forgive his illusion, then you deny him his real identity. Our inability to forgive holds the whole world back. All problems are illusions and when we fight to hold on to these problems we continue to fuel all of the false stories of the world. Forgive, so that both of you can be saved. See the world as playing a role, a mostly unconscious one. The lines were written by unconscious people. The plot makes no sense. Notice your conflict and ask yourself who in his right mind would create something like this?

Real forgiveness, real problem-solving, doesn't have any cost. You don't sacrifice your position. True forgiveness is a gift because the false position will be gone in both of you, like little devils exposed to the light for the first time. When you finally feel at peace, the point of further defending the false is gone. There is no price to pay or struggle to live through in order to see the truth. There is only a price to pay and a struggle to live through if you choose to see the false, mind-made positions.

Can you be done with the world before it is done with you? Can you see its madness and the madness of your current identity? If you can it will bring you clarity and purpose. One of the ways to get to this point is through detachment. Release your mind. Einstein said that humans will have to find a *new* way of thinking if they are to survive. Notice how he didn't say that we would need better technology, or faster progress, or better thinking to survive. He said we would need a completely new way of thinking. He saw that even if we made our old ways of thinking better it wouldn't help. There must be a new way, and that way is to align your mind with life and thereby get a new mind. Watch your thinking so that the new way of thinking can emerge through you.

This can only come from the realization that there are different levels of consciousness within us, and that levels much higher than our ordinary state exist. Jesus, Buddha, as well as all othe great teachers and avatars of the past were able to remove the obstacles which prevented them from their higher natures. As Plato famously wrote, the ordinary mental state of man can be compared to that of a prisoner chained in a cave with his face to the wall. On the wall are thrown the shadows of real things outside the cave. The man watches the shadows on the wall and believes this to be real life. The only way he can realize the truth of his situation is by turning himself around.

We must stop living solely inside our mind-made stories. If there are people still here in 100 or 200 years they will not be living and thinking as we do. Our stories and our roles must change and we must stop living in our world of shadows and fears. We must stop all of this destruction and war over our limited resources, when we have unlimited energy and potential within us. We are full of love in one moment and blinded by anger the next. Any challenge that confronts us, no matter how small, triggers an unconscious series of events within us and forces us to completely forget ourselves and our actual goals. We forget our thoughts of peace and prosperity and instead we run toward negative emotions and moods. This occurs many times during the day without us even realizing it. These small problems that confront us create our world, and soon we grow to believe that the world consists of these problems. We become incapable of seeing anything else or of extending any actual control or mastery over our inner states.

When we stop playing roles we allow our authentic higher nature to emerge in all circumstances. We are designed to operate from this state, with endless love and harmony, because this is the one truth within us all and it has no opposite. In reality, everything has very deep connections and nothing is separate in this universal fabric. This is why scientists use the term "fabric" when they refer to the universe – everything is part of the whole. Not even humans are separate from this fabric. For some reason we have an illusion of separation, fueled by our stories. We close ourselves off with anger. We are all connected; we are all part of the same energy field and living system. Choose to see this connection. Choose to get out of your destructive identity. Crack your old reality and begin to awaken. If you have a desire to do this, it will be done.

Lesson 12: Today know that only love is real. Give yourself space to watch and allow the truth to emerge through this space.

CHAPTER 13

Unification

You do have a purpose for being here, just like the rain, plants, and animals. Where do you think this comes from? When we discover the answer, it will be wonderful; pure happiness. We only struggle when we fail to realize our purpose. This is the key because most of our actions are driven by a false purpose which we have assigned ourselves. We think that our main purpose is to build or to do something, or to accumulate more things. We even believe that life doesn't know how to make this stuff better without our input, which is how we justify our need to struggle and figure things out.

When we find our real purpose all this means is that we let life speak to us again. Things become easy and the struggle is gone. Life gave us a purpose and of course we will fulfill it, and not only that, but it can be our happiness to fulfill it. It's why we're here. We must let go of all other purposes, all other stories. Life wants to give us only happiness and we must stop getting in the way. We deserve happiness.

In our own guilt we have listened to the ego and we have chosen to see ourselves as separate, alone, and unworthy. This dark noise obscures our holiness. We must tell ourselves often that life can only give us love and happiness because that is what *it is* and all other things are there simply because of our misperceptions. All we need is a shift in consciousness or perception. Then there will be the real self to experience things going forward.

Many of us have heard it said before that we were created in the image of God. If we believe this, then love created us and we are love. This isn't an emotion that swings from one end to the other. For example, in a typical relationship love turns sour very fast and that's not the kind of love we're talking about here. An emotion has an opposite but the reality of who you are does not, because the truth has no opposite. It's the truth and that means it's the only thing that is real. It's your internal condition, the truth of who you are and why you're here. At first it might hurt to examine this condition, but each of us must look within.

So if we say that only the truth exists and the truth is love, why do we get angry with things that happen in this world? When we learn to see the truth we no longer perceive things that aren't there. Anytime we are agitated, we are listening to and acting out our own stories. We are not connected to the source. It might take some time to connect, and everyone has a different path, but we must stay strong. If we really want to see the truth, if we're tired of the stories, then the truth will come to us.

Whenever a strong emotion comes over you, try to stay empty and merge with the field of pure energy. Let it pass through you. Don't go with it, don't go against it, let it be a puff of air. Let it pass and don't hold it there and accommodate it into your story as being for or against it. Initially you might experience pain and discomfort when you do this, but soon the emotion will pass through you and you'll see that you're still alive. You didn't need that story. And not only are you OK without it, but you're feeling great. Why did you ever hold these emotions before? Emptiness feels so good and free. Why constrict yourself and constrict life? Remember that you are what allows life to be, and your level of consciousness determines your life. It's not meant to be small. Nothing is small. Everything is vast, impermanent, and part of life. It is what *it is*, and it will help you recognize yourself as perfect, loving, and kind.

There are no mental abstractions that we must struggle to achieve in the outside world. We don't create anything; we simply allow it to manifest. Our true nature allows us to see everything perfectly. Everything simply *is*. Our old stories and perceptions don't need to be here anymore.

Why do we waste so much mental energy labeling everything all the while there was nothing we needed to label? In reality, we just needed to be happy vessels for life to manifest in this world. Why did we classify and work so hard to do things which we labeled as "good" and then punish ourselves when we didn't reach our goals? If we want true success, we need to let go of our perceptions as much as we can. We are already perfect, and life has a beautiful purpose for us that it will fulfill eventually. All we need to do is become still, stop thinking, and be present. Then the highest intelligence, the truth, will shine through us and guide us.

Anger is seldom warranted. And chances are the story you are trying to fuel with your emotions isn't even one that you want to hold on to. If you could see your true purpose, of course you would choose to let go of your anger because you would realize that any negativity only pushes you away from the truth because anger and negativity imply a belief in a false story. The fact that you haven't done so means that you have been choosing unconsciously. You haven't been choosing at all because you've been asleep at the wheel. Don't blame yourself or feel guilty. Move on and awaken. That's all life wants you to do. Many of the highest saints, such as St. Teresa of Avila, have accused themselves of ungodliness. It takes a certain level of humility to realize our unperfected human state and to not allow the guilt to prevent the ascension.

Be thankful for the journey you've made thus far because it has helped you to deepen your understanding of consciousness and of what you are capable of. It was something new and life is always experimenting, but now it's over and something else can emerge. Once you get your identity from life, instead of from your own stories, you will allow it all to be.

The ordinary use of our minds must be abandoned. The intellect and senses alone cannot reveal God to us. And what else is left for us to discover? We must evolve and reach the final stages of what it means to be human. Evolve, or else be left to suffer through a life without meaning. Return to the unknown. There are many methods but only one destination. There is nothing else. Every step taken away from it is a step taken toward unconsciousness. We will never be able to fully comprehend God because He is part of the invisible, the uncreated. However, we can come to know Him fully when we empty ourselves of all else, of everything that constantly ties down our minds in the manifested world. We can only experience this, we cannot conceptualize it. We must start *being* and stop trying to answer *what* we are and just realize *that* we are. This is experience in the raw. This is life without a filter.

Again, we must not place any guilt on ourselves because that is simply creating more unconsciousness. We interpret the best we can given our current level of consciousness. When we can't see the truth, of course we will be mistaken. We will be trapped in a reality that is not there. Such an experience isn't easy for anyone and unfortunately most of us are living this way. But anger and any other negative emotion such as anxiety, worry, or fear, can all be transformed into our spiritual fuel. Any time we feel them arising, we must take a look at why. What are we choosing to believe? What story or condition have we identified with? Can we let it go? Then we can repeat this process again and again whenever these emotions come up.

This won't be easy, but if we can do it, we will be free. These negative emotions will be sign-posts of what we need to work on and to let go of and we can thank them for guiding us. There was nothing we needed to learn. We needed to look within; to unplug our useless connections in the brain, the unconscious automatic triggers and stress responses. We needed them at one point in our evolutionary past but now we are unconsciously run by them and can't seem to turn them off.

We must let go of our worldly beliefs, goals, and interpretations. This is what Jesus meant when he said, "Do not store up for yourselves treasures on earth, where moths and vermin destroy, and where thieves break in and steal. But store up for yourselves treasures in heaven where moths and vermin do not destroy, and where thieves do not break in and steal. For where your treasure is, there you heart will be also."[1] These stories aren't permanent and they will be destroyed or stolen at some point.

The only thing that is permanent is your inner purpose and it is the only real treasure that can bring you happiness. How many times have you achieved some goal, or went on that vacation, and you weren't happy? You were so sure that you would be. Your only escape from such disappointment is your real purpose instead of the small one imagined by the untrained mind. Do not fill up your head with more small imagined goals. Let your goals and your interpretations go. Embrace silence. Let go of anger. Make this your purpose so that you can live in truth, love, and perfect peace. You don't need the small shell of this story to protect you. You don't need to struggle to make any special identity for yourself. See illusions for what they are and don't believe what your mind tells you.

What does your mind tell you? It uses language to create some sort of role. This might be a nice role, or a not-so-nice role. I am this or I am that. Based on this, my behavior, thoughts, and emotions will nicely fit into my assigned role. This is why the Buddha was so detached from the outside world, as was Jesus detached. They saw that our outside world was simply a misperception of our minds. We created these roles and gave ourselves a purpose that we were never meant to have. Therefore we live in madness, how can we not? Look at our operating systems. People have chosen to believe their conditioning. But no one can deny you your freedom. And your real freedom lies in discovering your true identity. Once you do, you can create your life the way you want it.

Power, creativity, magnanimity, and peace will all come when you free yourself from conditions and roles. You can still be a mother, father, doctor, architect, or whatever you wish, but it will be done with a different energy. You will no longer be molded and subdued. You will be given love by your higher self so that you can thrive and flow with life. Your life will not be unconscious and useless, but it will help people to live with lightheartedness, spontaneity, and joy. You will manifest your highest qualities and fulfill your ultimate destiny. You can still learn and enjoy the fleeting things of this world, but you will no longer take them so seriously. And you will use all things and roles as an expression of divine love and peace.

Can we let go of our need to control and allow ourselves to explore freely and safely? Can we become compassionate people, understanding and fulfilling our real needs? Otherwise what would be the point? To live a life dedicated to fighting the disease which we have created? It is time to dive down deep and create a new way of life that mirrors our true purpose.

The unconscious workings of the mind need to be brought to light and this is exactly what life will give you when you choose awakening. Don't be discouraged, be thankful that you are strong enough to face these emotions and to see them for what they really are. You can walk past the false and reach the universal mind; the mind of consciousness. What a beautiful and brave thing to do. To dedicate yourself to this is to realize your essential oneness.

Use your suffering, it is your key. St. Teresa of Avila wrote in *The Way of Perfection*, "If you love Him, strive that what you say to the Lord may not amount to mere words; strive to suffer what His majesty desires you to suffer... Let's give Him the jewel once and for all." Life has given you a beautiful gift and with it you can finally see past all of the noise and unlock your potential. Then you'll realize it was never locked to begin with.

Lesson 13: Today you have taken the first step toward sanity and cracking the false outer shell of yourself. Finally, the higher self will have room to emerge.

CHAPTER 14

The Big Adventure

Michael Singer wrote in *The Untethered Soul*, "What are you doing with life? This is what death asks you." You must face your fears in order to transcend, similar to the way of the cross. You change, life doesn't change. Only your relationship to it does. After you allow your old self to die you will be reborn.

Some might object and say that this doesn't fit in with our current scientific understanding of things. But our scientific understanding is very limited. Concept upon concept isn't the truth. The outside world is labeled, and words are labels of labels. In truth, we don't understand most of the nonmaterial world around us, which makes up 99.999% of our material existence.

How can we say we agree with the basic statement of science that "nothing can be created or destroyed" and then try to create and destroy? In the strict physics sense that statements ends with, "but it can be converted to energy." Einstein somehow equated mass and energy, and we can interpret this to mean that we are all reused, converted particles, molded energy, continuously and infinitely experiencing ourselves in form. As Alexander Pope wrote in *An Essay on Man*, "All are but parts of one stupendous whole, whose body Nature is; and God the soul... All discord, harmony not understood; all partial evil, universal good."

Can you still study planetary motion, or the human genome, or new medicine? Yes. But from the point of view that you are the consciousness that perceives all of these conditions and allows them to be. Without the filter of the brain, all would be atoms and molecules. Of course we need this filter and it's a pleasure to use it, but let's use it for good instead of letting it use us. Let's use it to fulfill our true purpose, instead of denying us of it.

For both good and bad thoughts, pay them no mind. Watch them come and let them go on their way. They cannot take you anywhere you need to go nor do anything to you that is real. Maybe they can shape the outer mold of you, but not the truth. No matter what you do in this lifetime, you can't change the truth of who you are. Seen in this way, guilt serves no logical purpose. This is wonderful news, but it can also be terrifying if you're heavily invested in the outer world. Don't wait until you're on your deathbed to discover this truth and to forgive yourself. God is in charge, and in order for Him to work fully through you, you must surrender all speculation. This can be summarized in three words: *watch your thinking*. Reject even the most exalted human wisdom.

Where does dissatisfaction in old age come from? The inner light of consciousness is still there. This inner light is the same no matter what age you are. When you were five years old, you could feel the light of your consciousness very strongly. Look at children and the joy and aliveness bursting forth through them. They are fully in the now and they are able to express themselves freely. Life is all about learning, enjoyment, and play. Then, as we grow into "responsible" adults, this light becomes very dim.

Actual responsibility would mean that we are in control of our inner states and our emotions, when in truth we're not. When we're no longer connected to this light, we suffer. We become alienated and depressed. We live our lives conforming to lies and working toward things we didn't consciously choose. But no matter what age you are, you can always reconnect with this inner light. No matter how weary your body may be, when you connect with your inner light you feel the joy and aliveness radiating throughout your entire body. Then, even in your old age you'll simply feel like a five-year-old that by this point inhabits a declining form.

Only you can choose to silence the voice in your head and to wake up from your false dreams. As it has often been said, the truth is paradoxical. We think that living in the present moment will make us dull, when in fact it will make us brilliant. We think that worrying about the past and being anxious about the future is necessary, when in fact it's completely unnecessary and prevents real success. You can still deal with things perfectly well as they arise in the *now* and realize that things are all right without your constant labeling, analyzing, and projecting. They're just things, after all, and without you there would be no one there to experience them.

As Plato said, "We can easily forgive a child who is afraid of the dark; the real tragedy of life is when men are afraid of the light." You are entitled to absolute bliss and happiness. Allow it to come to you. Open yourself up to receive. But how can you do this when the voice in your head is so loud that it sabotages any chance you have of hearing the truth? Become doubtful of what it's telling you. Be thankful for doubt. Without doubt you'd be the voice in the head and there would be no space for you to watch and remember who you are.

Doubt is the beginning of insight. And with doubt come many questions, and as the reality of your old purpose falls away, you might become frightened. Try not to analyze things too much and accept that they will be revealed to you in time. You might even find yourself becoming angry because you realize for the first time how little control you have over your own mind. Make use of this angry determination. Ask yourself, *Why can't I let go of this? Why am I holding on to it?* If you want to be free, you need to let go of everything that isn't the truth. You need to become free of forces outside yourself.

When you begin on your path, you are a child. Children have fragile, eggshell-like minds. They are sensitive and absorb everything around them, both good and bad. They are not strong enough to stand up for themselves. Sometimes you might still find yourself believing in struggle and playing out your old roles. Don't be angry or attack yourself, because this will only feed your false mental programming. Allow yourself to remain open and full of love and in due time the old patterns will slip away. If you continue to have a hard time letting go of your old identity, don't worry. Guilt will only take you further away whereas forgiveness will lead you right to the core of truth.

Lesson 14: Today you have decided that guilt isn't real and it has no purpose for you. You now choose to act consciously, relying on your own inner power. Each day you are getting closer to connecting with your authentic self and you know that this path can only be traveled in love. The experience of love is the language this transformation speaks and you cannot understand it in any other way.

CHAPTER 15

General Principles

"We are all failures – at least the best of us are."

-J.M. Barrie (author of Peter Pan)

Look at a cloud. What was it before it became a cloud? We know it was water, maybe part of some lake or ocean, and before it became water that very same hydrogen and oxygen were part of something entirely different. Of course it's not a cloud forever. That is not its permanent identity. Nothing on Earth has a permanent identity. We have manifested as humans out of millions of elements which were never born and will never die and were not so long ago part of something else. This is *oneness*. Everything we see is a temporary manifestation, a game of form, coming and going.

If we want to talk about physical or "real" things, then we can only speak on the level of atoms and molecules. Niels Bohr, the great Danish physicist, said "everything we call real is made of things that cannot be regarded as real." Under a microscope, atoms and molecules are the only "real" things we've got. All other things we perceive in our world are the result of mechanisms in our minds which have been designed to see things in a certain way so that we could perceive matter and inhabit these forms on Earth. Everything is subjective, and our minds were built to allow us to experience bodily materiality. If you think about that for a moment, could there be other minds that were built to perceive in other ways? If there is other intelligent life in the universe, then it probably isn't using its brain in the same way we are. It is probably much less focused on the 0.001% limited physical reality. It might be seeing the same atoms and molecules, but in different forms, hence the existence of different dimensions. It has evolved to see things differently, just as we will. And if this is the case, then who is right? It sees one thing, due to the clarity of its consciousness, and we see another. No one is right and no one is wrong because all we are doing is perceiving form given our *current level of consciousness*, and truth and perception are two different things. The truth is the same for all of us, but perceptions will differ significantly because it is more interesting that way for life as it is now lived.

Don't be too attached to these perceptions, especially when they have gone horribly wrong as they have for so many of us. Some authors speculate that there are many different dimensions of life, and many different levels of consciousness, and that we are continually evolving and moving through them. We are all here to better ourselves and to evolve, whether we realize it or not. If we don't realize it, we will be stuck in our current, low state of consciousness. But if we do evolve, we will go on to unimaginable heights.

This is why spirituality is here for us. We have misunderstood the meaning of life and death. Life on Earth is a brief experience of form. Then in death, our spirit is liberated as we return to the eternal truth and go on to have more adventures in form as we continue to evolve our consciousness. The most important thing we can do is to give ourselves space and become light enough in order to perceive this truth. Those that are the most trapped within their given identities, be they good or bad, are the furthest removed from this truth.

There is a show on Amazon called *Creative Galaxy*. During one episode the teacher was asking the kids to sit still and paint still life of fruit baskets and other such things. The kids kept running around so the teacher asked them again, kindly, to just sit still. But of course they didn't because they wanted to fly around the room. Then the teacher tried another approach. Since the kids couldn't sit still they decided to action paint and splatter paint on the canvas instead, similar in style to Jackson Pollock. This is a wonderful example of being fluid and recognizing *the need of the moment*. If the teacher had chosen to stay with the *perceived need* of following the agenda and painting still life, then it would have been a different episode entirely, one about obedience and painting fruit baskets. But if you're in the moment and you're enjoying it then you're able to be flexible and to adjust to whatever the moment brings. You are able to flow with life in the present and this makes your evolutionary journey much easier. Art class is supposed to be a recreational and relaxing activity, just like life. Try to adjust to the moment instead of always forcing the moment to adjust to you; and remember that it's all just a school.

Children get told to sit still all day long. Adults sit for nine hours per day – that's more than we sleep. We need benches everywhere we go so that we can take a break. We teach kids stagnation and it leaves us exhausted, too exhausted to tap into the unlimited energy within us.

When Jackson Pollock painted, he expressed himself though action. When you look at a Jackson Pollock painting you see a mess that is somehow alive. I'm sure that when he was painting he was able to bring comfort to himself. Likewise, when we ignore spirituality, we ignore our most immediate and mysterious need, the relief for all of our afflictions, our prime source of comfort. As long as this need remains unmet, there will be dissatisfaction. And this ignorance is innocent, because we simply fail to make the necessary association.

This is self-improvement not in the sense of material gain or knowledge. This is self-improvement for the sake of fulfilling our divine purpose and realizing ourselves as consciousness. This will govern every aspect of life and all will be transformed. That is how important and precious the spiritual path is. What Jesus did, you will do also, just as he intended when he said, "Very truly I tell you, whoever believes in me will do the works I have been doing, and they will do even greater things than these, because I am going to the Father."[1]

Stop giving your energy away in the service of futility and return to your true self, your indwelling higher nature. We have equated God with a belief system, and unfortunately many religious leaders have only taken us further away from the truth. God is a transformative experience because He is the realization that you are meant to be like Him, here, now. It is so much more than a belief! You either awaken, or it is meaningless and you continue to live in illusion, separation, and suffering.

What has prevented us from knowing consciousness? Mostly it was our own ideas of culture and refinement. Cultivation is achieved though likes and dislikes, but the true self is quiet and is beyond all of this. Many have spent years building up falsehood and then countless hours in maintaining it. As long as we continue to cling to this, we will not be able to know the truth, and spirituality will be meaningless. Only our false sense of self requires our constant mental activity. The very fact that it can't survive without our attention should prove its falseness. We are the necessary observers who interpret and create material reality – nothing can exist outside of our perception of it. Yes it's hard, but yes we can let go of our likes and dislikes. They are comfortable sometimes, if they serve a purpose. But unfortunately we have been serving them unconsciously.

Lesson 15: Today you realize that everyone lives in his own world, based on his own perceptions and current level of consciousness. The way you think is completely different from the way your child, mother, or friend thinks. You become still and you magically find your common language, the one without words. You are one with life and you allow consciousness to guide you.

CHAPTER 16

The Benefits of Emptiness

All roles turn into grievances eventually. When we forget our vast identity and cling to our small self we create unnecessary suffering. You can probably handle letting go of your negative thoughts and not taking them personally, but what about all the other, more comfortable ones? You might wonder *Will I still be able to think loving thoughts? Aren't they beneficial?* In order to defeat the army of bad thoughts, we must continue to strive toward the empty perfection which will manifest the inherent brightness of the soul.

Love and peace aren't really thoughts or emotions because they are not anything we create. They are our natural state, a gift that was given to us, and they can manifest in this world through us when we strip away the false. According to A Course in Miracles, when we awaken we live in a world we did not create and think thoughts that are not our own. They belong to the higher power living in and through us, the 99.999% infinite space which is who we are. To allow this shift is all we need to do. Then we can happily partake in the game of life and enjoy things as they come, and continue to enjoy them as they go. They won't control us anymore. Nothing can possibly alter our sense of self once we've glimpsed the truth.

Useless opinions, and even worse are useless emotions, burn up energy and take us further away from the truth. There is a deeper intelligence within us that can perfectly well take care of everything. If we think stress or anger is warranted as a solution, we will only create more problems for ourselves in the future. In any near-death experience, the survivor will usually say that he stopped thinking. Instead his body instinctively knew what to do. This is the intelligence that is within us and wishes to come through us into this world. Let's make this our purpose and try to implement it the next time we find ourselves in a stressful situation. Let's try to stop thinking and become aware. The peace within us has already taken care of everything.

Most of us live very stressful lives. No matter how we feel in the morning we are expected to get up, get dressed, show up and go about our days the usual way and act as if nothing is wrong. Our society likes to keep things the same. We are surrounded by routine with little room left for spontaneity of any kind. This makes sense because this is how the ego would rule its small and limited world. And before the new consciousness is able to come into this world, we will see the ego continue to dominate more intensely within the individual mind. However, eventually this will prove to be self-destructive for the ego because the pain of living in this world will simply become too great. We will return to ourselves, look within, and allow consciousness to emerge. A Course in Miracles teaches that there was ever only one problem and there is only one solution. Namely, to awaken and allow the shift to occur within that engages the higher power. And why is this power always described as high above us, as in the heavens? Because here on the ground, we are small, busy, and limited. But when we soar, and watch it all from above with detached awareness, we merge with the infinite and empty space of all that is.

The world right now could allegorically be described as the battle between good and evil, or awakening and unconsciousness. Evil has usurped the throne, but we all know who will be the true victor in the end. We are all rooting for the good guy, and this battle is actually within each of us. This conflict creates the world in which we live. Most bodies still inhabit a state of perpetual inner conflict driven by the emphasis on material constraints. Once this is over, and we are able to liberate our higher natures from our bodies, then we can once again inhabit our bodies peacefully. We will ascend to heaven once we remember the truth, and then come back down to Earth in order to bring this beauty here. Nature will not give up on us, she will keep trying. We are like toys in a workshop, or wood to a carpenter; constantly being molded and cut away so as to finally achieve our perfection.

Now is the time when nature and the universe will try again. We will take our inferior, earthly existence, and unite it with our superior, heavenly identity. Our birth and death, ascent and descent, happens as we purify ourselves upon this path. We live in a world of time and believe that heaven will come upon the completion of a series of events. But the truth is that heaven is already here, God is already present on the very dirt beneath your feet. Look at all of the wonder that He has created, and compare it to the mental noise within you. Look at the chaos of the cities we live in and compare it to the perfection of nature.

What if Buddha and Rumi and other enlightened people were right? What if death was never meant to be something to be afraid of? What if we've had it backwards this whole time? However, the majority still wishes to remain in this dream, and they are not yet ready to see the truth. Although this world brings them great suffering, they would rather die to protect this illusion than to open themselves up. They have become hopelessly dependent on this mechanical way of existence, so accustomed to hardship that any other reality is not allowed to manifest.

We must become aware of the resistance within us and stop unconsciously fighting to protect the very thing that is enslaving us. We have achieved such great advances, but the one thing that still plagues us is our lack of control and understanding. We know our life span is very limited, we will die, no matter how much we try to deny it, and we know that this death is not up to us and that we are not in control. We must learn to use this earthly death to achieve our own spiritual pursuits.

Buddha and Jesus both taught us that death isn't real. Christianity is founded upon the belief that Jesus was able to reverse biological existence and rise from the dead. And yet, instead of focusing on the resurrection, we focus on the cross, on the heaviest and most brutal part of life. But if we switch our perception and focus on the resurrection, then death isn't real. If we accept this to be true, then Earth can't be our home (because death and impermanence exist here). And if the Earth isn't our home, then our home must be elsewhere and we're temporarily experiencing ourselves as material forms. We are pilgrims, and our true home lies in the mysterious place from which we came and to which we will return.

Only one thing here is certain: there is nothing to be afraid of because what can be seen with the naked eye isn't the ultimate truth, in fact, it is the smallest part of the truth, it is a fleeting experience. The only way there is nothing to be afraid of is with the certain knowledge that the part which we can't see is an improvement on that which we can. Yes, the world that we live in obviously exists, but it is only a tiny fraction of who we really are. It's time to stop worrying and to die to the limited identities which we inhabit. The little self is only a manifestation of an abstract idea. This is why all of the great spiritual teachers taught surrender, forgiveness, and acceptance: basically anything to get us to stop thinking and fueling our misguided personalities so that consciousness can finally emerge.

The truth is that there are two entities within us: The earthly being and the heavenly being. So far, most of us have been attached to the earthly, the regular human life filled with limitation, suffering, and delusion. It's hard to let go because at least with the earthly being, although there is pain and suffering, there is an accompanying set of beliefs that are familiar to us and we pretty much know what we're getting. We fail to see that there are many different levels of consciousness, or ways to experience life. We not only fail to see this, but we actively blind ourselves so as to deny upward freedom and mobility. We are so consumed with our current state of affairs that we fail to realize that there is a spectrum of consciousness from which we can choose to live. This is why people differ so greatly, from sinner to saint. They are identical – their only difference being their chosen level of consciousness, or the way they perceive and interact with the world.

When you begin to cross over to your higher nature, false comforts disappear. You inhabit a space that cannot be identified with words, it simply *is*, but to your rational mind this seems like a dark and empty wilderness of death. It takes great courage to abandon the mind long enough to go there. When you abandon the ego you relinquish control and subject yourself to the will of God. Jesus referred to this when he said that

"By myself I can do nothing; I judge only as I hear, and my judgment is just, for I seek not to please myself but him who sent me."[1]

To get to the heavenly throne we must surrender and have the courage to walk through the wilderness of "no mind." The world is full of illusion, subject to dozens of laws. Illusion implies bondage to form and giving the outside world the ability to affect and to have power over us. We must become stable in our knowledge of our higher nature, and thereby transcend all mind-made illusion.

We cannot get to this realization with the thinking mind, which is rooted in this world. There is a common misconception that when we stop thinking with the ego we are automatically filled with "knowingness and infinite bliss." When this doesn't happen, and when people experience the pain starting to surface, they automatically flee because they think they are not doing it right or it simply does not exist. We must be patient and remember that it took Buddha seven long years to achieve enlightenment, and Jesus was in his 30's when he stepped out into the public eye to preach his message.

Lesson 16: The Dali Lama said, "When you talk you are only repeating what you already know, but when you listen, you may learn something new." Be silent and listen to what is happening within you.

CHAPTER 17

The Thinking Mind

"Can we stop the stars from hurtling across the heavens? No. We cannot stop the mind, either. Off it goes, and then we send all the faculties after it."

-Teresa of Avila, from 'Interior Castle'

So how do we change the world? We let it be. If we try to use our distorted words and minds to solve things, then we will only further remove ourselves from the truth. Jesus said that it was not him, but the Father working through him. Buddha said to surrender the self. This is what we've heard over and over and yet we've never wanted to do it.

Upon closer examination, our words tend to be unreliable. In Nazi Germany a "criminal" was someone who stood against the Nazi regime and the brutality they imposed. The collective unconscious distorted things to such an extent that even German religious leaders pledged to follow the ideas of Adolf Hitler as a symbol of hope.

This is how subjective the ego can be, and it will distort and erase until all that you see is what it wants you to see. The collective pain in Germany made them do horrible things. All rights were taken away. Many were possessed by this thinking entity which was being fueled by a bruised sense of national pride, and few were awake enough to see the truth of what was occurring.

We must be able to realize that everything is God. Love is already within everything because it is the code with which all of life is created. Don't allow the level of thinking that is limited and full of anger and suffering to control your mind. If something is alive here on Earth, it was made with love, and it is love. This is radical because it implies that there is no need for grievances, separation, or limitation; we just think that there is when we choose to believe in the illusions of the ego. We must open ourselves up to accept wealth and abundance and choose God's will as our only happiness. We must surrender everything to God and actually put what we learn into practice. Our human identity must become empty, and then it will be full of space, energy, and intelligence. We must become present enough to enjoy the journey and to never worry. We will sacrifice nothing, because letting go of a delusional ego is nothing to grieve over.

Self-knowledge may not be easy to attain, but we must not turn away from the hard work involved with introspection. The alternative is to struggle to hold on to the pain of the past. We won't need it anymore because we don't need to be punished. We just need to awaken. We must surrender all grievances and know that we will be healed. That's it. Then we focus on the now and we make sure to watch our emotions and inner dialogue with detached awareness so that we don't accidentally get swept up by them again and sabotage our own wishes. Then happiness, right-action, and solution-consciousness will freely live within us and guide us. Everything will be new and different.

Imagine talking to your neighbor or family member or someone at work and letting his or her form-identity fall away. The form identity doesn't garner all importance anymore. Although you can still see him or her, now you will be able to see past the form. You will be speaking with another spirit from elevated ground. You have glimpsed the divine. You even find yourself doing this with people you used to get upset with because God is now in everything and you are happy and content.

Both the human part of you and the spirit part of you need to come together. If you're overly attached to the dense human identity of Joe, 47-year-old male, dentist, then you're not aware of the vast spirit within. You can serve and help others to awaken once you balance both the human and *being* parts within you. You don't need to live in a world of stress and struggle. Can you accept that these are not your natural states? And more so, can you see that they are against the wishes of God and life? How could we have glorified these states before? Can you accept that this isn't what God intended and that we were mistaken? Isn't it easier to admit that we were wrong, instead of choosing to believe in a reality of suffering? We don't need to feel guilty for this; in fact we should be glad because this is salvation and atonement.

Everyone is here to teach you a lesson but first you need to be silent and still in order to hear God. Watch your thinking. No true spiritual teacher has ever told you to think hard and to figure it out. Instead, they told you to be still and surrender yourself and your thoughts. Stop fighting to hold on to them and let God's voice become louder so that you can finally hear it telling you that you are both part man and part God, just as Jesus was. He came to show us the path for our awakening. Higher consciousness is full of peace and there is very little thinking involved because the solutions are able to emerge through us with ease and clarity.

Oftentimes, the mere thought of other people gives many us of anxiety. When we go to walk our pets or visit the grocery store, we hope to not run into anyone. But A Course in Miracles tells us that other people will be our salvation. God speaks to us through other humans, they are all in our lives for a reason and the angrier that they make us feel, the more we need to learn from them. A strong negative emotional reaction to someone is indicative of a very big lesson that the ego doesn't want us to learn and it is trying to blind us with strong emotions in the form of anger so that we don't accidently hear the whisper of truth in the background. The good news is that these spiritual lessons are free and occur quite frequently throughout the day. We can make tremendous progress simply by following this spiritual practice and living harmoniously with others, no matter what the mind may say about it.

Once you learn to place yourself on the path toward happiness, life will become more peaceful. Some people will leave your life, or the relationships may become transformed. Either way, you have fulfilled your purpose. It may be terrifying in that moment to stop believing what your mind is telling you and to become still. Many people who have been practicing yoga for years are still unable to carry that mental state of stillness with them after they step off the mat. But that's the big miracle. That is what you need to do as your spiritual practice. It's that easy. Forgive and be here in this moment because it is the only place where God can be found. God is within everything, and everyone around you will teach you a valuable lesson. As more and more people awaken we will finally return to our state of grace before the fall and before sin and judgement.

Christ Consciousness, or Buddha Nature, or whatever you wish to call the state of perfect bliss, lives within our human form. We need to take good care of this form and pay attention to it because it is our doorway. This is another paradoxical truth: The form you inhabit isn't the real you, but it is a way for you to become aware of the real you while you're here on Earth.

If there is a difficult situation or grievance in your life, ask, What do you want me to do? Please move through me so that I may happily fulfill *your* will, for I know this is no accident and I am no victim. I wish to stop judging myself and my brothers and to receive freedom and peace for myself and for the whole world because I know I cannot give what I don't have. Let me not place any guilt on myself. Let me feel your peace and your love, for "thine is the Kingdom, and the Power, and the Glory, now and forever. Amen." Notice again that the word is *"thine"* not "mine." This is why we must settle down and let go. We were never meant to create anything on our own, with the limited brain that is unaware of the energy which it contains. We were meant to allow creation to come through us. We are simply vessels for God. We are made of empty space for a reason.

Now, this is nothing to get upset about. It doesn't mean that we have no control over our destinies. No, of course we do. God gave us free will. Unfortunately most of us have used our free will to enslave ourselves and create suffering because we think we deserve punishment in the eyes of God. God made us in love, just like everything else in His universe, and no matter what we have done this truth cannot change. Our purpose here on Earth is to remember to be love, and only this purpose and the fulfillment of it can bring us happiness.

Our actions will be happy and our lives will be happy because we will be aligned with our center again. We must let go and relax. We were meant to create something much greater because it's something that is not of our small self. What we allow to manifest through us here on Earth will be miraculous because it will not be done by the lower self, but only through the will of God. We must remember that we are simply the vessels and become still.

God is in everyone. Remember that no matter how horrible someone may appear, he has fallen asleep and is under the grip of illusion. Or, he may only appear horrible because you are under the grip of illusion, or limitation and suffering. Shake him, and yourself, and wake up. Don't make him feel any worse about himself or yell at him and force him into a deeper sleep. And don't place any guilt or judgement upon yourself. Remember you are unlimited. You are not this material form, because it is only 0.001% of who you are. You are the 99.999% infinite space of energy! If you really want to change the world and yourself, the way to do that is through love. All we need to do is wake up because we have been overly identified with our tiny human function and have temporarily forgotten about our massive spiritual capabilities. We can only awaken with love, and then we can move further down the path of perfection.

Consciousness wants to awaken within us so that we can all be at peace and remember our true identities. Through forgiveness we achieve heaven on earth. Jesus didn't ask people to come to church and listen to him. He asked them to do as he did. He asked them to become as he was. He asked them to heal and to save themselves and others. He wasn't preaching ideas and opinions; he was giving us the truth about life and our purpose.

The Bible is a highly metaphysical text, meaning that it is above the physical. This is why Jesus spoke only of love and forgiveness, because these qualities don't belong to the limited human mind, they are part of the infinite. He was trying to get people to let go of identification with their false and limited material roles. Once the false is gone, then the beautiful truth of God can emerge on its own. People will either understand and embody

Jesus' teachings, or his teachings will be meaningless. He was only concerned with the direct application of his word. Turning the other cheek, as well as the story of the son who squandered his wealth, were all meant to point the way to directly realizing the Christ within.

Higher consciousness will either come out through you and into your life or it will remain as the words on a page. Jesus' vision of the new earth is realized once you merge with Christ consciousness. This consciousness is your gift because it is your tool for remembering and embodying God here on earth – and it has been placed inside you and will shine through you as soon as your old self, the one listening purely to suffering and delusion, dies. There is no one who will come and do it for you and there is nothing you must believe intellectually. This is something you must become and it will transform all parts of your life. You must choose to do it today, right now. The ego has hidden this from you by making you think that there is someone who will come and save you, or that there is another goal you must achieve in the future. Salvation cannot be found in time; in fact, it is the use of time that keeps you away from salvation. The truth can come only in the here and now. Freedom and peace can come only when you remember who you are and let that identity shine forth into this world.

You cannot be hopeless and you cannot sin once you remember who you really are. Such notions become meaningless. The truth awakens the whole soul. Salvation is within you, the new earth is within you. You must take this responsibility upon yourself. Let's choose to drastically transform our lives and the lives of many generations yet to come. This sounds like such a big job, and to the small and limited ego, it might be. But the blueprint for this realization is already within us. Once we decide to look and download the instructions, the arising consciousness will be able to fulfill this through each one of us, one step at a time. This is our purpose.

We can continue to choose our opinions and play out the roles which we have grown accustomed to, or we can choose the truth. Opinions are created by time and roles can only live in time. We can let go of the past and the future and choose the present. It doesn't matter what we thought or did previously, and we don't have to worry about the future. Any worry means that we are disconnected from God and any plans made in such a state will only lead us further away from Him.

Miracles will come from this surrender, this detached watching, and the realization that everything that isn't love is an illusion and so it can change. And it will change, because everything we need in order to bring this about is already within us, right now. Each of us holds a different piece of the puzzle. We need to heal one another so that we can transform the world. If anyone is hurting, we know that we have not fulfilled our purpose.

Again, don't think about how large this all might seem. Just look within yourself and ask yourself what is your part in all of this. What does consciousness wish to manifest through you? In *The Art of Possibility*, Benjamin and Rosamund Zander wrote, "Life takes on shape and meaning when a person is able to transcend the barriers of personal survival and become a unique conduit for its vital energy." Just let it happen. This truth will quickly change everything. You will positively help everyone around you. Remember that your purpose is to allow consciousness to emerge through you into this world, to rid you of the false image of you and replace it with your perfection. The Hindu spiritual classic, *The Rig Veda*, states, "It is man who is all this, whatever has been and whatever is to be."

The truth cannot change, it is everlasting. If the outer world was the truth, then we would all be in big trouble. Luckily, it isn't. The outer world is malleable and will be shaped and formed until it fully mirrors and reveals the truth of our inner world. When this happens, we will see things differently. If enough of us accept this mission as our new lifestyle then the shift might happen rapidly. If not, then it will happen a little slower. The important thing is that we decide to start this today.

The way we intend to look at time and space, absolutely everything will be different. We will grow in our depth and understanding; it will be like living in a whole new dimension. Instead of just our three-dimensional reality, there will be another vastly higher one. This spiritual dimension will allow us to see in ways and to do things which we cannot even begin to imagine.

And yet, this is our birthright when we realize that we are as God created us. This is what we are here to bring about. This is why many spiritual teachers say to watch from the space of emptiness, or the 99.999% infinite energy that you are. Who knows how long it will take, but we must plant the seed now. In celestial time, there is no time. There is only the *now*. It is written in the *Rig Veda*, "*Stay right here* – do not slip away, but stay unwavering, like a mountain. Stand steadfast here... and here uphold the Kingdom." Remain with your awareness fully in the present moment.

Who knows what else there is in the universe? Maybe we'll finally be able to think and understand things with our new consciousness which will allow us to travel further and connect with other life. Of course this can be labeled as science fiction, but maybe it is closer to the truth than we would like to admit. The way we are living our lives now oftentimes seems more unreal. How can we continue to believe we are so small?

It was less than a decade ago when the best writers of science fiction coined terms like robotics, time travel, zero gravity, warp speed, droid, nanotechnology, clone, virus, and space time in their stories. Now, all of these words are part of our scientific world. The website *Dictionary.com* created a slideshow titled: *10 Words Coined in the Sci-Fi Universe*. In it, they wrote that the word "robotics" originated in 1941 with the sci-fi writer Isaac Asimov, and the word "time travel" has been around since as early as *The Mahabharata,* one of the two major Sanskrit epics of ancient India, which H. G. Wells later elaborated upon in his stories. Arthur C. Clarke coined the term "zero gravity" in his first novel, *Sands of Mars*. The term "warp speed" refers to traveling faster than the speed of light while inside a space craft. It originated from the Old English word *wearp* which refers to threads running over fabric. It became a popular in the 20th century to describe space and its relation to time as a fabric.

From this, it would seem that our fantasies play a vital role in creating our reality. But of course, such a belief would take us off the rational path, and lead us toward the magical or mystical. The funny thing is that if we were more open to the magical, then our scientific world would profit immeasurably and we would be able to make advances which the rational mind cannot even begin to grasp. To turn toward the magical doesn't mean to turn away from science and technology – it means to open ourselves to much greater progress in these fields.

To become a modern alchemist, to be able to perform a complete transformation in your life, you only need to remember one thing, the main teaching from A Course in Miracles: Anything that isn't love, isn't real. An alchemist is able to take whatever comes to him and transform it into what he desires, which is always in loving alignment with the truth of the universe. This is how you are meant to live, too. Whenever there is a problem, welcome it as an opportunity to love and to practice your transformational skills. Just like an alchemist, call on the universe to help you figure out what lesson you need to learn – and then move on. Give the problem as much love and light as you can, then focus on the present moment and open yourself up to receive better things in the future. The only thing you need to do is to clear your own mental baggage so that you are once again able to receive.

Does this sound too good to be true? Is there a voice in your head saying you don't deserve it? Turn down the volume of that voice and focus on the part within you that is elated because you finally remember the truth. You only have one purpose, and that is to let God's love manifest through you.

This has two implications. First, to assume any other purpose is extremely selfish. If you choose to believe in any negative thoughts or to remain a victim and focus on the problems of the personality, know that you are putting your own purpose above the one that consciousness has for you, and you are focusing on less than 0.001% of reality. Second, the purpose that the universe has for you will come forth through you effortlessly. Any time there is struggle, or attachment, it is a sign that you are trying to solve this on your own. This is a very impersonal process, in a good way. Beautiful things come through you. You watch and enjoy them and all the while you are centered in *being*, in God within. This is true for all of us. Remember that consciousness loves you and wants to evolve though you.

Let all other things fall away.

There needs to be balance between your center in being and your actions as a human in this world. You need to be grounded and focused, and you also need to be open in order to allow the universe to manifest wonderful things through you. You have been limiting yourself. Now that you know the truth you will begin to manifest such wonderful things; things you couldn't even imagine before because they come from a much higher source and they are not of the small you. Resonate with the highest frequencies and you will live in a world that consciousness creates for you. Remember that you are merely energy.

We will set things straight and we will remember the truth, and in so doing, we will transform our relationships and our world. We will choose love. What we give will come back to us. Through compassion and forgiveness, we will learn that we don't have to fight to change anything. We just have to love. The answer was always that simple, and we intend to hear the true message of God.

Lesson 17: Today you choose to be one with life and a blissful servant of love. With this knowledge, you are free to surrender in order to stay open, positive, and flexible.

CHAPTER 18

Ignorance

"You are the flower. Rarely found and beautiful beyond measure, you are also vain and selfish. You often allow your pride to get in the way of your true feelings. Despite this, you are truly loved and treasured."

-The Little Prince

By this point, through your reading of this book and application of the lessons, you have seen what most never get to see. You have become more peaceful and you see that the typical human life has been clouded with unnecessary suffering and misery. We are fighting every day to keep the "truth" of our outer world alive. It's chaos. These conditions will continue to show up in different forms as long as we continue to listen to the limited voice of the personality. Why is it so hard for us to choose love? Why are we afraid to try and see what happens?

Our greatest achievement would be to reach a point where we are able to not think, to stop being completely identified with our malfunctioning minds and to create space for the voice of truth and beauty to enter. The mind is like the driver and we think that we are in control this driver, when in fact the car is running wild. Even if the driver (mind) tries to communicate, after all these years of unconscious living, it will be hard for the conscious mind to get the body to listen. Our body and emotions are not interested in awakening.

Our bad feelings and unconscious tendencies are like wild horses, pulling our carriage (the body) every which way, and the poor driver is not in control of anything (so long as he remains asleep). Our carriage is built for life many years ago, when it wasn't civilized and the roads were rough.

Now, we are still trying to function in the same rusty, clunky carriages, when the roads are paved and perfect – we just haven't realized. There was a point when we needed to have tough bodies and minds for survival, but life is much lighter now.

Even when we are alone and washing the dishes, the voice inside will still regulate us and tell us that we're washing the dishes. Of course we are! We don't need to have a mental dialogue about it. But worse yet, if it isn't labeling what we're doing in the present moment, it will be busy worrying about the future or being negative about the past. Then a wave of anger might come and we have no idea where it came from. Our mood shifts as all of the cells in the body listen to the lies of the mind and off we go. This is mostly lower level consciousness, although it can be action-based, but both states are very impersonal. These thoughts did not originate in us, but they need us to think that they did in order for them to remain alive and eat away at our energy and sense of self.

If we believe in war, then we believe in the world as it is. If we believe in peace, then we believe in pure and perfect consciousness. Jesus constantly told us to release the personality and to not be so attached to this world; to stop building our treasures here. We are confused in terms of what our treasure, meaning our purpose, really is. Our opinions change constantly. The only way to reach the truth is through unconditional love and peace, meaning to realize the other as yourself, and love him or her.

Every moment of every day we are choosing who we wish to believe in: the small, temporary personality, or the deepest truth in the universe. We constantly hear people talking about the one life that we are participants in and most of us have been unable to grasp the true meaning of this. It isn't something that can be understood with the mind. We must let go of all of our notions, grievances, and limitations. Then we can feel this beautiful oneness. And of course once we feel this oneness we can continue to achieve things in the outer world. In fact, for the first time, we'll be in love with it! The actual path, the doing, will become wonderful.

When we can let it go it will come back to us in its true form. It's a spectacular playground and love is everywhere we look. Obey the word of God over the delusional inner voice. As A Course in Miracles teaches, "Let truth replace all illusion in your mind." This is a metaphysical text and we are living in a time when we are finally able to scientifically explore the truths of the reality which we cannot see. As Bohr said, "If quantum mechanics hasn't profoundly shocked you, you haven't understood it yet." For the first time, science is able to offer support for many of our mystical claims.

The perfect frequency, or the highest level of consciousness, is already within us, ready to emerge once we surrender the false. It doesn't require visualizing events, it requires surrender. Even Nikola Tesla said, "My brain is only a receiver, in the Universe there is a core from which we obtain knowledge, strength, inspiration. I have not penetrated into the secrets of this core, but I know that it exists." Getting to this core involves *allowing and surrendering.* In this way, the ego is finally banished because the results will not come from us in any sense. We realize that we are simply manifestations of spirit. We don't realize this truth now because we allow matter to reign supreme and we are presently inclined to suffer against our own impurity. We must decide to take on the necessary work to free ourselves.

Einstein also once asked a fellow physicist, only half-jokingly, if he believed the moon is there only when you look at it. The atoms and molecules which make up the moon are microscopic. If you were to take all of the matter that makes up the human race, and remove all the space between the atoms, we would all fit into one sugar cube, because atoms are 99.999% empty space, meaning pure energy. Since we are made up of atoms, this means that we are 99.999% empty space, which is not empty at all, but is full of pure energy which manifests itself as the world that we see. Our sense perceptions merely give us messages, and we create our entire world out of these messages and ideas. Something happens within our minds which manifests as the seemingly real matter in this world, and what that something is, the code which creates the reality of our world, we know not. But even when we hear this, it is extremely difficult for us to understand the implications because we blindly cling to the seeming reality of our outer world. We fail to see that without the mind, without a conscious observer, nothing would be here at all.

We are vast and infinite and connected to all knowledge, we have simply forgotten this and decided to focus on the tiny, less than 1%, part of ourselves, which is the manifested form. Most of our universe is invisible to the naked eye, just as we ourselves are essentially invisible. Our minds create our worlds, and without our brains to interpret and make the picture, the atoms and molecules would remain as mostly empty space, as pure energy without form, and in that sense, they would not exist as anything manifested.

Bruce Rosenblum and Fred Kuttner, two physics professors and the authors of *Quantum Enigma*, wrote that "Einstein was bothered by quantum theory's claim that if you observed an atom to be someplace, it was your looking that caused it to be there – it wasn't there before you saw it." Science tries desperately to grab at a rational reality. Quantum theory, which is the physics behind one third of the products in our economy, pulls the rug right out from under them. They refer to it as a "measurement problem." But many of the core principles of science rely upon phenomena which cannot be readily observed, and without these abstractions the formulae do not work.

The main problem of the measurement problem is that we are actually creating our past right now, in our present. In the famous double-slit experiment, the photons passed through the fork as either waves or particles, and only after we observed them (which happened *after* they passed through the fork) did some act as particles and some act as waves. If we never observed anything then they would all be waves, meaning pure potentiality, but by actively observing, we altered the past and made some of the waves choose to behave like "solid" particles. This is staggering! Even Stephen Hawking is theorizing that our present is actively determining our past and that all linear time is simply a construct of the mind.

Quantum theory has, in its own way, actively discovered consciousness because the observer that influences the physical phenomena must be outside of the system, must be non-physical in nature. Science depends upon the invisible reality in order to describe the visible, even if it refuses to admit it. Do we have the power to create everything in our world right at this instant? Probably not, because it can more accurately be described as a *choice*. The observer, meaning you, chooses to focus on one specific thing.

Ultimately, Quantum theory tells us that what we measure influences what's out there because our minds string it together and animate it to create an outer picture. Science is supposed to deal with *understanding* this phenomena and how our universe was created, but instead science wants study the less than 1% of actual existence on the external level by classifying it. When our scientists try to assign physical properties to things which have none, it cannot be said to be proper. Ultimately, the main error of science is that it sees these facts through the limited, lower level framework and fails to apply them to the higher levels of thinking – meaning pondering the purpose of life and so forth.

Science has brought us to the very place which it is most terrified of going. Of course modern science, which prides itself on measuring and understanding the physical, will be afraid of leaving the "solid" world behind. We must understand that science, and our entire way of thinking, is currently very poorly structured and that a new way of thinking must arise, one that acknowledges that nothing can be found to exist outside of our perception of it.

What does this mean? It means that in a very real way, you are playing a part in the creation of all life around you at every moment. Life is just the incarnation of consciousness into a temporary form and you are one of the most highly conscious forms on this planet. This is why it is so critical to focus on *expanding* the consciousness that is within you instead of wasting your energy on outer events which were created by your consciousness in the first place.

To some, it would seem that Quantum physics is so outlandish to our normal experiences that it's unproductive to try and relate it to economics or anything else in our lives – and yet, it is the principal behind our lives. It is the study of the way life works, and like it or not, these are the answers our scientists are finding. Albert Einstein said, "It followed from the special theory of relativity that mass and energy are both but different manifestations of the same thing — a somewhat unfamiliar conception for the average mind." That which we can see is the same as that which we cannot see – the visible is simply a different, heavier, denser form of the invisible. Our visible world must be cherished because it is our key, our map, to the invisible.

Some physicists just like the idea of using their minds. They pay no attention to the shocking implications of their discoveries, that there is indeed a hidden hand, a single consciousness, without which all science would be meaningless. It is common for scientists to discover the most massively important thing, and to proceed to act as if it had no metaphysical meaning or implication, to focus only on the material use. This is using the mind as a muscle, without the underlying solution-based wisdom and understanding which would piece it all together.

We are finite in our desire to acquire knowledge. We focus on what we already know, and we build more and more upon concepts which are familiar to us. To actually venture out and discover information about something different would completely alter the way we live. We will not be able to truly know anything until we awaken. Without the higher wisdom of consciousness, our biggest mistake is often a lack of modesty in thinking our minds can naturally understand the full complexity of life.

The study of Quantum physics attempts to get to the smallest particle, some tiny material beginning to hold on to, but there is no smallest.   The big is made up of an infinite amount of the small – out of one, ten thousand things. The search for the "God" particle, which is the smallest particle, will go on forever. The vast space continues to break itself down into smaller and smaller parts.

We were so excited to grab the microscope because we thought that once we got down to atoms and molecules that would be it, but we were wrong, because even atoms and molecules hold tiny particles within them. Should we continue to spend billions of dollars building machines that we think will help us see this smallest, "God" particle? We continue to believe that the ultimate reality is somewhere outside of us, and so we search for this small material beginning which will explain everything. But this is not an easy task because the atom is a system which is infinitely complex and immaterial in nature, because just like everything, it perfectly mirrors the universe. So long as we continue this search outside ourselves, seeking into small tangible parts, we will not reach the ultimate truth, which is set to remain in the invisible mystery which surrounds us.

Instead, we need to focus on space, which holds an infinite amount of small particles. Space is everywhere. At the atomic level, the world is made up of 99.999% space. This means that the material world we see is less than .001% of the truth. It is like a small leak. If we could stop being completely identified with it and blinded by it, we could learn how to harness the deep truth, the pure energy within us.

In order to create the illusion of materiality, space is oscillating and the oscillations interact. You are spinning at this very moment, and the speed at which you move will depend on your level of consciousness. The higher your speed, the more conscious and powerful you are. The slower you spin, the more you are attached to the material level of struggle and smallness, and the less powerful you are. We spend a lot of time paying attention to that which we call matter, and we spend very little time trying to understand the space in which it abides.

Space is full of energy and information. This is why all of the great teachers of the past have told us to look within, because we are made of this space and this knowledge is within us, right now. Matter is the result of the division of space itself, and we are interacting with this structure every second. We are experiencing, learning, and feeding this information back into the infinitely dense field of space around us, and in turn it goes on to create a reality which tends to fit the common consensus. According to the findings of physicists, we are informing the universe about our specific points of view on the whole thing. We create our universe and our universe creates us. We are part of the vacuum that goes from infinitely big to infinitely small, through us. As it passes through us it picks up our specific interpretation of the universe and feeds it to the infinity of all things so that our participation is counted. We are part of the infinitely small and infinitely vast. We can connect with all knowledge because we contain it within ourselves.

The space inside the atom is full of energy and vibration. It is infinite and it is infinitely dense. Space is not empty, everything just cancels out and looks to us like nothing, meanwhile we're floating in and are sustained by this. Our life is almost completely empty space and infinite energy. And yet, the majority of us walk around complaining that there isn't enough. We even go to war for energy and resources because of our belief in the seeming reality of limitation and insufficiency.

Consciousness is in this empty space, not in the brain. The brain is just the telephone or radio, downloading the specific data; it is the vacuum which connects us to our material life. Seen in this way, the brain cannot be said to be the source of our existence. The brain simply figures out how to filter information into something that resembles our current perception of life.

If you were to present such findings 100 or 200 years ago, the science would not be there and people would not be ready to hear the truth. But again, facing the reality in regard to our planet and our future here, we no longer have the logical option of not believing. Quantum physics sweeps the common sense, material facts, right out from under us.

This is how evolution works: we are forced into it. It isn't easy, and it involves struggle and suffering in order to propel us to the next level. As Darwin observed, something, some hindrance, forced the fish to leave the sea and the birds to take flight. Now, we too must transcend. How much more pain, difficulty, and suffering must we go through before we are willing to take the risk and transform our lives and stop doing things that are not in line with our life purpose? Every person that chooses wisely makes a huge impact because we must remember that each life experience is counted.

We will create heaven on earth. We tell the space what we want, and the space works with us to create it. This is abundance. We must collaborate and find the center, the stillness within ourselves. The deeper we go, the more powerful we are. It is an exciting time to be living through such a collective awakening, but it is also difficult. Now is the time of change, change which many will oppose as they struggle to keep their destructive systems in place. But the Earth is highly unstable, and as Einstein said, we must find new ways of thinking in order to survive. We must connect ourselves with space.

If we succeed in connecting with space, then we will be able to have access to an infinite amount of energy. This would mean complete abundance and freedom from struggle. All that is left for us to do is to obtain this energy, or connect with consciousness. Enough of us need to awaken so that we can all find the solution on the material level, and tap into our infinite energy.

The following generations will have a much easier time, since this is how it has worked for the past 400 years. When Galileo attempted to disprove some of Aristotle's theories, he was labeled a heretic, but he persisted in showing his evidence. We no longer burn people at the stake, but nevertheless our minds find it hard to accept new information. Newton held on to his discovery of gravity for quite some time due to his fear of criticism, and also because he was busy helping his mother fight off accusations of witchcraft. Times have changed, but we still resist new ideas much more than we think we do.

Quantum physics teaches us that our observation of an object causes it to be there. If we take a minute to truly think about it, this means that the existence of anything in the material plane depends on us. However, this does not mean instant manifestation, at least not yet. Our machines have become so clogged that our observational faculties and senses are running wild. We currently have no control over the interpretations that go on to create our reality, but this does not alter the fact that the world depends on us and our interpretations.

Lao Tzu wrote that the rational mind is our biggest enemy because it is always cutting away and trying to understand. He wrote in the *Hua Hu Ching* (in the version translated by Brian Walker) that, "She who lets go of the knife will find the Tao at her fingertips." Our knife is our search for some rational, material understanding. Our insane desire to live in a world that does not depend on us and that has some other permanent reality outside of our perception of it. Lao Tzu was perhaps one of the first to understand how the universe works:

> ". . . These are notions of the mind, which is like a knife, always chipping away at the Tao, trying to render it graspable and manageable. But that which is beyond form is ungraspable, and that which is beyond knowing is unmanageable. There is, however, this consolation: She who lets go of the knife will find the Tao at her fingertips."

Scientists were slow in catching up, but they are finally getting there, as confused as ever, but finally admitting the truth of the great metaphysical teachings, and of the enlightened masters of the past such as Lao Tzu, Buddha, and Jesus. Our search began with a fixation on the outer world, a scientific study of observable phenomena. This made the truth appear to exist outside of us in a world that was thought to have a reality apart from us. We believed that if we were only able to explain the atom, then it would stop there. We would finally be able to say *There it is! There is the material basis which we were looking for!* That was the permanence we needed, but of course, we didn't find it, nor will we. The answers we seek are irrational.

No matter how outlandish it might sound, our mental and physical worlds are intrinsically connected. Isaac Newton himself said before he died, "I don't know what I may seem to the world, but, as to myself, I seem to have been only like a boy playing on the sea-shore, and diverting myself in now and then finding a smoother pebble or a prettier shell than ordinary, whilst the great ocean of truth lay all undiscovered before me." The great ocean of truth laid undiscovered before him, and this coming from a man who made the most tremendous scientific discoveries in history. His greatness came from his ability to see the smallness of the scientific world, and to sense that there is a greater truth which we have not yet begun to seek. Upon his death, scholars were surprised to discover that his notebooks were not filled with mathematical formula and scientific calculations: they were filled with his metaphysical interests. The smartest among us are the most humble, the most comfortable with their lack of understanding. Newton produced a complete change in outlook for us all, and yet, he admitted that he hardly knew a thing.

Lesson 18: Life is so good and you have all of the energy you need within you in order to enjoy every moment. A beautiful balance can be found in which you enjoy every moment and you feel abundant. You can still plan for the future but now that future can be aligned with what the universe wants. Now the world is pure light and it's so wonderful to be here in this body for this short amount of time. Time only passes by because of your awareness of it. Once you merge with this awareness, you become time itself. You are the present moment and everything in it. There is no more separation. Is any little belief or grudge worth sacrificing your truth?

CHAPTER 19

Salvation

Stay focused on consciousness. Whatever life throws at you today, take it with grace. Then your love can transform the situation. That's the only way it can be done. Every day is a day for transformation. It is an opportunity to surrender the seemingly real world and to look within. And it is in these little personal transformations that we will be able to transform the world, because we will awaken and our perceptions will be healed.

Make unconditional love and peace your only goals and be one with the life around you. This is the source of true power, to surrender the small identity and to align with the higher nature within. Once you are able to see the impermanence of this world, it becomes easier to look within and to examine your own perceptions. Let go of illusions and embrace presence. Be a radical source of peace. All of the most wonderful people to have ever lived have said that their power doesn't come from them. That is revolutionary. Imagine a world where people live in alignment with the thoughts of cosmic consciousness. This isn't just a dream – it can be a reality once we remember that there is a human aspect and a divine aspect that makes up who we are. We've all seen what the human aspect can do. Now is the time to examine what the divine aspect can do once enough of us link up with it.

In the old world, and still very much today, God was seen as God and man was seen as man. They were believed to be two completely separate ideas, when in fact, we are both. We must realize, as Jesus said, that God is within us. We must awaken our inner higher functioning faculties, instead of remaining asleep. We must differentiate the seemingly real, meaning our current world, and the seemingly unreal but actually very full and powerful inner world. We are both part God and part man. We can heal and create a new world with our new perceptions. That is how incredible we are and have the potential to be. We've simply forgotten it and decided to identify solely with the limited-man part of ourselves. When that gets to be too much, just remember that there is another dimension to you that is waiting for your desire to connect with it.

Life can be so good. You can see love all around you and you can give freely. You can enjoy every moment, feeling the life within you, and seeing the deepest truth. You don't have to live the typical human existence full of limitation and struggle. There is another reality but the first step is to realize that you no longer want to live just like everyone else. You want to connect with the deeper part of you. Once you have this desire, your heightened energy will take you to a place of clarity.

We may not be able to rationally explain what we find once we link up with the higher self. How could we? We are equipped with limited tools and we are trying to discuss the source of life itself. As someone once speculated, we were not placed here to ponder the truths of the universe, but to pick berries. The most wonderful gift is when you no longer feel like you need to explain anything to yourself. The Buddhist master Dogen wrote "Mountains do not lack the qualities of mountains." There is nothing you need to explain, you simply need to let it come through you.

Do not toil, do not spin, and do not worry. Jesus asked if being worried could add a single hour to your life. And what is worry? It is mind activity and the false identification with the seemingly real outer world of suffering. This is what you must let go of in order to align with the universe and allow it manifest through you. Jesus ended his flower allegory by saying that not even Solomon in all his glory clothed himself like one of these, meaning that once you align with life you will be more abundant than you could possibly imagine because grace surpasses all material things. This whole time the only thing holding you back was your own mind.

The human part of you might remain a bit confused at first and that's all right. This is the hard part: you must be comfortable with being uncomfortable and not being able to explain things rationally to yourself. For example, notice how you interact with others. When do you get upset and why? What situations are you still trying to control? Observing yourself in these situations will lead to a higher awareness of what you need to surrender to. If you criticize and condemn, you are unknowingly attracting those false qualities to yourself.

Our thoughts and reactions happen automatically which means that for the most part we have no control over them until we develop the higher self. Destructive thoughts are not ours alone because we all share this collective ignorance. A belief that served a purpose earlier is still being held within the mind, although it is no longer useful and has now become a hindrance. We unconsciously maintain these beliefs, some of them going back to a very young age. When we are able to notice this, we will finally be able to take back control. Then we can drop our collective identification and return to spirit. We have a choice of listening to self-deceptions or listening to truth.

Why would you hold on to delusion when you know you deserve abundance? And even when the human part of you is confused, the spirit part will rejoice at the awakening that is finally happening. It has begun because you finally have space, and slowly you can align with your true purpose. Don't let the old doubts, anxieties, and limitations of the human part of you creep back in to disrupt your higher nature. The real you has been trapped this whole time and all it needs is your willingness to let it out.

We consist of two parts, spirit and body. Our spirit is who we really are, whereas our body is reliant upon outer conditions and preferences. Our body is constantly shaped by outer events, and if we remain asleep, what this body chooses to see and do will not be up to us, although we might continue to believe that we are free and in control. There is no guilt; everything is now in our hands.

Now that we have begun the awakening process, for the first time we can consciously choose the truth. But even in the moments when we can't, and the old negative energy takes us over completely, we mustn't beat ourselves up. We must use it to learn. Do not blame the sick human part. Nothing it ever did could possibly alter the spirit, the living divinity within. Remember that you do not lack any of the qualities you need.

Lesson 19: Today we are consciously trying to connect with being. This part of you, and of everyone, comes from pure consciousness, and this is your true self. It is infinite and full of energy and your only job is to allow this to come into the world and to lift the veil of darkness.

CHAPTER 20

The Eyes of Immortals

You might see the truth in all of this, but on a daily basis you're not yet sure what action to take. Eventually you will be completely guided by your inner *being,* which is the voice or teacher within. You don't need to load your head up with plans. In fact this is one of the biggest deterrents to inner peace. You need to become silent enough so that thoughts can fall away and peace can arise. This peace will tell you what to do and your plans will be made and carried out effortlessly. This is the miracle and it will replace all struggle if we allow it. This is how we can attain happiness.

The old concept of atonement involves making compensation to a wronged party and is widely understood to be a process full of difficulty and suffering. We think we must atone for our sins, and this keeps us rooted in limitation. But true atonement is nothing more than present moment awareness, which means total escape from the past and total loss of interest in the future. Is a total loss of interest in the future supposed to be regarded as a desirable goal? Yes! Real compensation is heaven - here and now, in which everything else is wiped out.

So why are we not able to enjoy the present moment? What prevents us from placing all of our attention here? Why do we believe that suffering and hard work are a necessary part of human life? Jesus gave the parable in which laborers who arrive to work at the end of the day are paid the same as those who have been at work since sunrise. This means that we don't ultimately benefit from long, hard work, but that our true reward comes without this price.

Don't we wish to be peaceful and happy? Can we start by accepting the fact that we are not following our true function and that something is blocking it? Although darkness is also a part of the light and makes up a part of life, we don't have to consciously participate in it and suffer. We can allow it to be and shift our attention elsewhere.

When we place our attention in the *now*, we'll see what was always obvious: there is nowhere else. Although this statement is simple, it carries the full truth if we allow the mind to receive it. If there is nowhere else but here, can any of the elsewhere thoughts possibly be real? This is the root of all human error – the belief that the future holds salvation and the past is necessary for identity. A life lived in this way is completely devoid of truth. The mind has brainwashed us into identifying with it and using it non-stop. Now is the time to take back our power.

Any thoughts about the past, which are probably negative, remember that they aren't real. Any thoughts about the future, which are probably negative also, remember that they aren't real. Where will you be then? You'll be here and you will surrender to the present moment. You will discover the beautiful and wondrous play of life and consciousness all around you. Stop living through the old, highly subjective thoughts. The little person doesn't need to be real in you anymore. Let it see the light of truth and see if it can remain for long.

In the Bible, the release of suffering is often the way to heaven. Luke 21:28 (NIV) states "When these things begin to take place, stand up and lift up your heads, because your redemption is drawing near."[1] Luke 21 to refers to The Second Coming, which precedes the end of the earth, and it is in accord with our message because it will be the end of ego-based living. This means that during our association with sorrow, in the form of suffering of any kind, is the time to lift up our heads. It is the perfect time for us to choose space. We can choose to remain unconscious and allow the negativity to take us over, or we can remain open, receive a heavenly outlook, and be made whole.

Sorrow can crack the outer shell long enough for us to stop, look around, and be still, but for most this is easier said than done. We've identified with the collective craziness for so long that it unconsciously pulls us into complete obedience. The next time you experience anger, or maybe the loss of a job, or unhappiness of any kind, can you welcome it as a sign of the light coming to show you the truth? Ask this experience to show you a way out. Let this change be your miracle; be still and ask what you need to learn. If you can forgive the world and stop identifying with it, then you can awaken. With forgiveness, your victim identity dissolves, and your true power emerges – the power of presence.

Incarnation is described as the transformation of God into man. This transformation lands you here as a human being. So if somehow you can eliminate the human part of you, what do you think will be left? This is what is meant by the death of the self, so that only being, which is God consciousness, can remain. This is your purpose. All unhappiness comes from resistance to this in an attempt to keep the human alive. It is your free will to do so, but hopefully once you can fully see what you're capable of, you can step back and choose differently. You can choose peace and power again. Why again? Because that is how you were originally made.

But if you do remain identified with the sickness, the fall, the man part of you, then you will be given many future opportunities to awaken. Remember that Jesus spoke of suffering as the way of the cross, and Buddha said to surrender the self. There will come moments in life when things get so bad that you are finally ready for a different reality. Life in the human identity becomes unbearable. You can't tolerate crawling any longer because you know you are meant to fly. You are looking for the solution to all of this, because deep down you know this isn't right. But if you haven't yet become aware of the vast power of consciousness within you, then to step away from the man part tends to appear suicidal. Who will you be if you step away from the only thing you know? If we are unaware of being then such a choice is impossible to make because we don't realize that we even have a choice; we think the human is all that we are. Unfortunately this is what most people believe now and it will take a very big leap of faith for us to cross over into the truth.

All unhappiness comes from resistance because you want to keep identifying with the stories in your head which make up your identity. Your belief in them is very powerful, and they have caused you to become blinded and fully identified with the man part of you, or your fictitious human identity. This has caused you to take things personally, become a victim, fight, and struggle. If anything threatens our preconceived notions of human identity, then we become hostile. We unknowingly take on heavy emotional baggage for the sake of keeping our roles alive.

The good news is that these roles cannot survive without the energy of our participation, and this energy is no small amount. It sucks us dry. Look at a child; he is not struggling or giving away his energy to keep anything alive. He simply *is* and he doesn't care one bit what you or anyone else thinks about him. He is rooted in the *is-ness* of the moment. Remember, mountains do not lack the qualities of mountains. You simply are, and there is nothing you lack. All you need to do is just to be here in this moment and to love. Anything that requires your struggle to survive isn't real. It's that simple, and as long as you resist it, you will be holding yourself back.

As soon as you step upon this path, life will become magical and mysterious again. You will be humbled and in awe of everything, and how beautiful that state will be! Let all humans live like this now. Let the God part guide our actions, and the human part carry them out blissfully, without a care in the world, because the human part has become a vessel instead of an identity.

When you surrender your fictitious concept of self, you can begin to live authentically. Everything will be clear and it will reflect your true desire. You won't need to work at a job you don't enjoy, or say scripted things, because you will be able to live your higher truth and be completely free in your self-expression. Your outer life will be transformed due to your inner transformation. The truth will shine through you and you will happily rest within it with a clear and peaceful mind.

We are all here to help one another to heal and to remember. We should be open and malleable. However most people have their purpose confused and thus they live in illusion. They think their purpose is to create more stories, more businesses, more things to "better" the world. At no time do they turn their search to contemplate the only place that matters, which is within.

Consciousness wants us to have free will because it wants us to create lovingly. Once we "return to the master for instruction" we receive only love, and after that we can do whatever we wish. Consciousness created this majestic complexity, and it can create much better than the limited, biased, and poisoned mind. We are consciousness. We are not here to struggle the way that we do. Remember, if there is anything you don't like, use it as your spiritual practice. Go within and see where you have been mistaken. Let go of the purpose you thought was yours and embrace the purpose of life.

Our duty isn't to fight any wars for any ideologies. This is madness. Our only duty is peace. Let's focus on our similarities, believe in one another, choose the compassionate route, and heal the world. Once we are able to look around and to see the madness, we will no longer identify with it. We will be able to see that the struggle we were born into was never real, and that the outer world can be different. And it will be different, because it is our purpose to play, heal, and evolve. Just remember that none of it is permanent, so why live as though it is? Why continue to give power and importance to something that is so inferior? Why not realize that we've held the key to liberation within us?

We are all living with sick minds. We think the problem is out there in the form of a disease we must fight, or a competitive work environment we must struggle to keep up with. We think that we are doing great, that there are just a few small things we need to fix out there, and then all will be well. When we examine the staggering inequality of wealth, we have programmed ourselves to believe this is natural. That not only do we not need to help, but we must continue to strive to take more for ourselves. This all comes from believing that we are different from one another, and that these little forms that we inhabit are the truth. But if they were the truth, would we really need to struggle this hard to maintain them?

Who taught us to believe in death? This is the major trap which holds us.

Enlightenment is realizing that there is no death. You are a spiritual being in a body that you don't know how to operate. Your inner voice of truth, consciousness, or being, has been silenced. It doesn't know how to reach you because you are too busy. Remember, this was just a play of forms. None of it was meant to be your permanent identity. Nothing in this world has a permanent identity. Even time is relative because the only way that time can be experienced is through you. If you look at a photograph of yourself as a child, and then at another one of yourself as an adult, you will see that time has lived through you. It has expressed itself through your form, which is the only reality that it has. So why fight this? Why can't we see time as something that is experienced through us; that everything is experienced through us? Nothing would be here without the consciousness which is within. Life didn't appear in the universe; life created the universe.

The truth is that your real inner state is one of peace and joy. It has been temporarily covered by dark clouds which gain importance through the unconscious addiction to them. Nothing negative is real. However upon first hearing this, the mind will make it almost impossible for us to believe this because human minds have worked hard for thousands of years to make humans believe in the opposite of truth. This is where our vital life energy goes to on a daily basis, the constant maintenance and upkeep of illusion. This is the truth that the stubborn minds refuse to realize. If we stop for even a moment, we will be able to realize this. If any doubt about the illusion comes knocking then by all means open the door, or at least stop actively holding it shut.

The first step is to become aware of the negativity and roles which you hold on to. Try forgiveness and distance. Can you feel your inner light? This light wishes nothing more than to express itself through you and to guide you. You are surrounded by the treasures of life every day. You are life and you are complete, whole, and protected. You were not born here and you will not die here because you were made in the likeness of the Father. This is a temporary role, and it can be played with peace.

Coming back to the concept of atonement, this is why the spiritual path isn't an easy one. Most people cannot step back from everything they have been conditioned to believe. They would rather remain prisoners than to seek liberation. When we surrender and become still, for the first time we are able to consciously observe our inner state and the negativity that makes us uncomfortable. This unconscious pain has nothing to do with us, but it will make us believe that it does and this is where the big illusion comes in. We listen to it and we think that we are bad, so we seek punishment in the world. We think that the world can somehow punish us and thereby save us. That if we sacrifice enough, somehow that inner feeling of guilt and inadequacy will go away. But this is completely backwards, and most people have remained stuck in this.

The truth is that we are good and nothing in the outer world can ever add to that goodness. The truth is that the outer world controls us and makes us feel horrible because we unknowingly give it that power. The outer world is a weapon of the ego and we unknowingly imprison ourselves because we have forgotten about our good and believe ourselves to be separate from consciousness.

We have been placed in our bodies, which are basically highly sophisticated machines that we have no clear idea how to operate. It is pretty obvious that our bodies, our machines, are running inefficiently. We hardly yield anything of true value and if we were a factory or a business we would have filed for bankruptcy long ago.

It's just like the first time you got behind the wheel of a car, you knew it was dangerous so you took the time to learn. You didn't try to figure it out on your own. We should take as much care with our minds, instead of unconsciously assuming we are who we are and that the world has taught us the best. The truth is far from it. The world has taught us the worst and it lacks even the slightest amount of spiritual truth. We have been living with many years of mistaken actions. Although we are mechanical, our machines are by no means clean. Maintenance is required to clear off the debris from many years of unconscious living.

Our bodies work by receiving input from the outside world. Based upon this input, an appropriate response is selected from all of the variable reactions within us. If we receive a negative input, then we will produce a negative reaction. This is the inner cleanse that must be done – we have the power to transform these dense and negative inputs into light and beautiful reactions. We must stop wasting the resources of the factory in the production of coarse living, and focus on producing the lighter materials upon which our spirits thrive.

The only way to return to your higher nature is to unlearn. You must release your attachment to the world and to the mind which tries to imprison you every step of the way. If you watch a thought, you can see that in the moment before it is formed, there is stillness. Then as the thought shuffles in, if you are not careful you will identify with it, taking it to be your own.

The real you isn't the body, mind, or illusions which fly in and out and get you to identify with them. Remember that you have been placed in a highly sophisticated machine and you are finally getting a copy of the manual. You were so excited to drive this impressive thing that you forgot to read the instructions. You must go back for a copy now so that you can become your own master. Jesus, Krishna, Buddha, and many others read the manual. Freedom from compulsion, restlessness, addiction, and negativity of any kind are yours. Suffering isn't real – you just need to go to school first to figure out how to maneuver around it.

You have an incredible life force within you. Something is channeling energy so as to pump blood and keep you alive. Millions of cells within you are following a code. This code is the source of life itself. It has always been within us, but if we are left to our own highly unconscious devices, we will blindly forget about this life force and instead focus on the illusions of the outer world. If we forget about this light, then we will not be able to produce the health and happiness which we all seek. But, if we are able to awaken, by dragging ourselves away from this illusion, we can produce the miracles we need. It is interesting that we must drag ourselves away from such false identification, instead of willingly embracing the truth.

Who wrote this code? Where did it come from? Scientists cannot say. This code is consciousness and it is who we are. Scientists are barely able to study the outer effects, let alone the origins. It is so complex, that it has taken us thousands of years just to build up a rudimentary understanding of it.

If we fail to understand ourselves and our own processes, we will remain slaves to our insane bodies and beliefs. If we fail to accept the work of self-actualization, we will continue to remain the subjects of forces which we perceive to be outside ourselves. But the worst part of all is that we will fail to recognize that we are in prison. That we are trapped. If we remain in the limited state we will continue to believe that we are free and that this limited way is the true way tin which life should be lived. In such a false perception of reality, we will have no desire to escape because we will be completely blind to the fact that escape is possible.

The solution is simple: return to consciousness while you're here. Pay attention to the instructions. This is the only thing that can keep you sane. Stop driving blindly and experiencing the world through your limited and blocked senses. Without self-mastery, you will never be truly free.

Lesson 20: *Identify with consciousness, which identifies with nothing. It is part of everything, it is part of time which expresses itself in all things, but it has no permanent identity. Release your attachment to your out-facing mind and return to the pure sense of self.*

CHAPTER 21

Change in Being

When you are fully focused on things, then you are completely identified with the body. This means that your responses, desires, and actions will be those of a typical human. If something doesn't go your way, you will get mad. If someone cuts you off at the intersection, you will take it as a personal insult. This is the typical human existence of someone who never took the time to check the manual and is reacting blindly to the conditions of the world.

The solution is the death of this false, conditioned entity within. If we were deprived of this false entity, then there would come an emptiness which would cause the collapse of all illusions. This collapse of our desires, goals, dreams, and fears would finally allow us to experience being, which is our simple and pure reality without any outer attachments. And then, for the first time, we would be able to rebuild and to choose for ourselves what we wish our lives to look like.

The other part of you, consciousness, functions at a higher level. It chooses to manifest forgiveness and compassion. Gandhi functioned at this level, as did Jesus, Buddha, Martin Luther King, and Nelson Mandela. They fascinate us because they have transcended the human dimension and are expert drivers on the roads of life. They bring beauty and peace into this world. This is what everyone is intended for, but if we remain identified with the body and the outside world, it will be closed off to us. We are all born with the same consciousness. It is our job to discover it and to let go of everything else.

Consciousness has always been and will always be, even if we remain unaware of it and believe that people like Gandhi are special and separate from us. They are not. They have gone through many of the same trials which we have; only their response has been different. Instead of holding on tighter and believing in the seeming outer desperation, they let go and took the time to accept responsibility and to read the manual of consciousness. This is the highest action and will align you with the most powerful energy, which is all that you need in order to bring your best self into this world. The solution, the highest possible dimension for you, is already here. All you need to do is to align with it, and to stop believing in desperation, death, and illness. Allow that level of illusion to diminish within you by watching it and not giving it any more of your energy, then naturally you will be guided toward good action, wisdom, and peace.

The typical human is unaware of the higher dimension and thus feels very limited and doubtful. If your life seems full of limitation, misery, and lack, then you are predominantly functioning at the level of illusion, in which any solution is virtually invisible. The certainty and unlimited clarity of the higher levels aren't available yet, but as soon as you are willing and ready to awaken, they will be. They exist equally within us all, but most have not been able to attune themselves in order to receive these transformative frequencies. Much like a television, it must be wired and tuned correctly in order to broadcast the perfect picture. All of the different waves and frequencies were already there, but before the invention of the television we had no way of using them. This is similar to the higher dimensions within us. They are within us already and nothing can possibly alter them because they are our birthright. We can only choose to deny it, and unconsciously choose our own personal beliefs and stories of what life should be, and thereby manifest a picture of that which we don't necessarily wish to see.

Our primary purpose is to connect with higher consciousness. Only when assume this to be our primary goal, and use every moment of life as our spiritual practice, can we bring about miracles. A miracle is simply a manifestation of a law that was previously unknown and invisible to the naked eye. Based on this definition, a miracle would constitute most of the material world, since we are only able to perceive and to understand a small portion of it.

When we are connected with consciousness, there is a beautiful peace that emanates from us. Buddha referred to this as non-doing, which means that although you are sitting and doing nothing, many things are getting done which you might not be aware of. Then when it is time to act, your action will be powerful because it will be aligned with life.

We have a mind that cannot grasp the vastness and connectedness of life. In fact we hardly know why we're even here. If one little thing is off inside our highly sophisticated bodies, such as the loss of eyesight, we find it very hard to function. For the most part, we hardly know anything about the bodies we inhabit, and yet, since we deem ourselves to be smart enough to build cars and toaster ovens, we have confidence that we are already aware of everything – or at least, the "important" things.

However when we wish to connect with higher consciousness, life becomes wonderful. Of course we will still do things, drive our cars and make toast and achieve whatever we like, but it will be done with peace and purpose. We will finally be in control of the highly sophisticated machines we inhabit. They will no longer be in control of us, and we will be at peace – or at least slightly more relaxed.

When we fail to connect with higher consciousness, the busy activities that we engage in are used to keep our illusions alive. This is true for those who realize it on their deathbed and wonder why they wasted their lives. The busy ego dies at some point because it is part of human life. For one living lives solely in the ego, in the end they may come to realize that none of the things that surround them actually mean anything. They didn't connect with their purpose, which is consciousness, and thus missed the point of existence. Their life was full of illusion because they weren't connected with the everlasting.

We must not be afraid of inactivity. This is one of the main mistakes. The ego has labeled inactivity as laziness so that it can continue to keep itself alive. Inactivity can be our gateway to consciousness, provided we do it in an alert and awakened state. We don't want to sit around and fall asleep, which means that we would drop below the level of ego or thinking. We sit, and we watch. We listen to what is going on within the body. We ask ourselves questions about our identity and our purpose. We do whatever feels right and we travel deeper into ourselves.

Most people spend their days arguing over just the tip of the iceberg. Dive down and see the great depth. You'll be awed at the life which you were unaware of. You were focused on the tiny tip, but the great depth tells us that no matter what happens at this tiny tip, there is so much more to it. This is a miracle and a blessing, and you'll want to share this vision with others so that the whole world can be improved. Your work, your relationships with your friends, children, and family, will all be transformed. You will be one with life, purpose, and consciousness. Say goodbye to old doubt and limitation and the crowded life at the tip of the iceberg. Dive down deep and know that sacrificing this tiny tip is no sacrifice at all. You can still visit life at the tip of the iceberg and you can participate in it but now you are a happy visitor because you have taken up permanent residence elsewhere. You still create, but now you do so with ease. You can still travel and eat and have wonderful experiences, but you do so without undue longing and attachment. You are free.

Remember that what your body labels as laziness is one of the main guilt traps that the unconscious mind uses. First of all, you must become aware enough in order to notice this and to prevent yourself from fully identifying with it. Resistance can often come up when we are pursuing our dreams. This is the ego trying to prevent us from being happy and achieving our purpose. The way to bypass this is to see what it feels like to not do the action. Do you feel like you are missing a vital part of yourself? In your ideal world, if you could do anything, do you see yourself doing this? If so, then practice awareness. Become still, watch, listen, and forgive. Connect with the depth of life. Soon you will be able to overcome the resistance. The resistance will melt away because it cannot survive in the light of your awareness.

Remember that resistance is found at the lower levels of consciousness, along with suffering and delusion. To struggle with it is what it urges because it is hungry for your energy. Remember that there is nothing you need to struggle against. When you do what you love, it is effortless and right action is what brings you happiness. You are one with life. First and foremost, forgive yourself and be happy that you are finally connecting with the truth. Everything that happened formerly was necessary because it has gotten you here, but now things will be different. Heaven on earth is real, very possible, and it happens right now.

The body and mind have been trained in darkness. They see limitation and lack. If you remain attached to the thoughts in your head and the outside world and believe them to be real, you will continue to experience failure. This illusion will create more struggle and failure for you. Remember that this outside world is shaped by your level of consciousness and is a reflection of your inner state. Of course it is real in the sense that it exists, but you have permitted yourself to be consumed by it, mostly unconsciously, and you can change it because you are the *observer* and this reality depends on you.

Remember that your outside reality is composed of vibrating atoms and molecules. Everything is energy; our minds just aren't equipped to see it that way. Also, everything comes from one consciousness. Even the "bad" is an expression of this consciousness, at the lowest level, because there is nothing else. This oneness makes up your body, your thoughts, and the outside world. The outside experience for most people is madness, and it is a direct reflection of the inner state of the ego. The body and the world didn't come to you with an instruction manual. You were born here with the hope that you would remember where you came from and use this earthly experience to enjoy yourself and further expand your consciousness, moving ever upward toward the perfect higher state. Then, in the fullness of time, you would return home. Unfortunately, for the most part this hasn't been happening. Miscommunication has taken over the body, and fleeting experiences have incorrectly assumed themselves to be who we are.

We search for ourselves in things that are limited and of course they can never tell us the truth of who we are. We ache to be limitless because we feel trapped and are aware that we are so much more than this. Our limits are optional. Relax the mind until the truth reveals itself. A limited mind and a limited environment will not show us this because they cannot see it; at the limited level, solutions do not exist, only problems do. Only the real you, which is the highest level of consciousness, can see this.

This is a choice you must make for yourself, but remember that once you do so, your mind and environment will try to pull you back in for a while. Don't listen to them. A change in consciousness isn't easy; but stay strong and tell yourself that you want to know who you really are and why you're here. You want to live with the peace and wisdom of the higher planes of existence, which is solution-consciousness, perfect action, and being. You want to be unlimited and certain. Why else would you be here? Who do you help if you suffer and create more unconsciousness?

In truth you are the formless space which allows all of this to be. You are something beyond all words. You are a part of everything in the universe and you can continue to live in this tiny and wondrous speck of dust called Earth, only now you know the truth. You no longer fully believe in the words and stories of others. You recognize the truth as you listen to Jesus and become meek, which means quiet and still. He wanted us to understand that we are just like him, meaning that the Father is within us.

Jesus said that we would go on to do even greater works. He did not die, and neither will you. This is the salvation and the truth. *You shall know the truth and the truth shall set you free.* If what you believe is limiting you in any way, then it can't be the truth. The truth is light and beautiful! The truth can only be love.

Let go of self-seeking desires. There is no need to inflate your ego further. There is a difference between wanting a home for your family and wanting the mansion on the block. There is a difference between wanting to have a nice career, and wanting to gain high rank. You are permitted to have desires because they connect you with life and time. But these desires ought to be fun. They ought to serve you and enable you to enjoy a new experience. They are not meant to be all or nothing, as in, if I don't get this promotion, or buy this, or go on that vacation, then I'm nobody. Life is already perfect and complete and it comes in many different forms. Just enjoy it and don't take anything too seriously.

Jesus never said that you must work hard to build up your identity while you're here and struggle the entire way. He knew that the way we were living was polluting ourselves. Much of what was said was misunderstood by later interpretations of the Bible. Jesus found the unlimited when he connected with the source of life and love and abundance. God wanted us to be fruitful, but he made sure to tell us that the only way to do so is to surrender in faith and to realize that we were placed here to be fruitful. We are grapevines, and we can only bear fruit when we listen to our inner instruction on how to be beneficial grapevines. A grapevine doesn't try to take over the world. A grapevine bears fruit effortlessly because that is its natural function.

That's why Jesus also speaks of trees that don't bear fruit as being useless. Of course you have a purpose for being here, and it will manifest effortlessly once you deepen your connection with higher consciousness. It will bring you happiness to fulfill this purpose. What we think of as work, with all of the struggle and effort, as well as the stressful environment, is not what consciousness had in mind for us. We are here for a purpose. We are here to manifest something wonderful. We cannot manifest anything wonderful when we feel limited and full of guilt.

We have suppressed ourselves to such an extent that almost everything we do goes against our nature and the will of God. Every day is meant to be full of peace and abundance. This is how we must teach our children to live, and we can only do this by setting the example ourselves, no matter how tough it may seem. Eventually, it will get easier, and it will be even easier for subsequent generations.

Manifesting is beautiful. It's wonderful to bring something into this world and to connect with others. The spirit within you is so special that it carries the instructions for manifesting something so unique and beautiful that it is not of this world. You don't have to think about anything because this realization will come to you through faith, not through your thoughts. You will experience love in the actions you take, and in witnessing the manifestations coming forth into this world. This grace is so mysterious, the only way to connect with it is to let go.

Your current identity has many likes and dislikes because it lives in separation. The best way to begin to undermine this identity is to yield whenever you catch a wave of strong emotion coming over you. Maybe you had a long day at work and you come home and your children are being wild. You want them to be obedient and quiet and this causes you to lash out at them. Then at night, once they're in bed, you feel guilty because you really love your children. They are the reason why you go to work and try so hard in the first place. You are in bed after this episode and all of these thoughts and emotions are running through your mind and you close your eyes. You feel the pain and chaos within you. You watch what the mind is feeding you, as if you were just some innocent bystander. You concentrate on feeling the inner body, the legs, the head, the feet. You begin to relax and you realize that all of this is just a story. You believe you must work at your stressful job and you believe your children cannot naturally behave themselves unless you lose your temper. You accept this. You don't try to sugar-coat it or give yourself excuses. You don't try to cover it up with positive affirmations. You just watch it. This gap in thought and emotion, this temporary letting-go of identity, has created space within you and you are no longer fully identified with the voice in your head, or the ego.

Remember that since you are able to watch this mental/emotional process within you, it cannot be who you really are. Just as in Quantum theory, here too the observer (you) influences the observed (the world). There are lower and higher levels of the observer within you, and the level you choose will create the world that you see.

So the next day you wake up, and you try to continue this practice. You are careful and you *watch* as much as you can. You get down to the most primal level as the observer. You try not to think. You realize that your thoughts never actually came from the real you. They were running on autopilot.

Lesson 21: Try to create as much space as possible and soon you will feel peaceful. You will choose peace and you will choose to see the light. You will build up enough courage to connect with your true self and your purpose and your life will be transformed.

CHAPTER 22

Miracles

When you are *alert*, you pay heightened attention to everything around you. And when you are *still*, you are able to watch yourself and ward off unconsciousness. This example has been given often, but it's just like the sky. While you are thinking, think of these thoughts as being clouds that block the sun (your true self). Even light, beautiful clouds still block the sun, and dark clouds are heavy with water and need to empty themselves through the form of an unpleasant situation.

Don't get caught up in either good or bad thoughts, which come as light and dark clouds. Remember your identity as part of the sun, not some passing cloud. Both the light and the dark wish to manifest themselves, but it is up to you to choose which level of consciousness you wish to be a vessel for. When people awaken they begin to notice all of their negative thoughts. They think they need to replace them with positive thoughts. But the ideal state is lightness, which is free of thoughts, either good or bad. Then the sense of self is blank, tranquil, and alive.

The mind knows that alert stillness signals the end of its madness and destruction, both within the body and the outer world. Switch from *doing* to *allowing*. Instead of learning more, try to unlearn. Empty yourself, become peaceful, and let your natural joy come into this world. This will guide you and your life will flow with ease. You'll no longer need to waste energy on frivolous pursuits and stories. You can watch. And when the time comes to act, you can do so, and it will be powerful. Remember to let go of the little self.

Sometimes what holds us back are labels and words. It's hard for us to release the past because for so long we've believed all of our limiting thoughts to be real; but remember that the word real can be deceptive and means different things to different people. How real is the world that we live in? From one point of view, it is very real because we are able to perceive it with our senses. From another point, it isn't real at all because without the senses, it doesn't seem to exist. Under the microscope, our actual bodies completely disappear. But our limited senses don't let us see this. Just as a house is built from an *idea*, or the vision of the house which the architect holds in his or her mind, we completely lose sight of the idea, which is of primary importance, when we focus on the bricks and mortar. Our lower, grosser senses reign supreme, and the higher functioning is completely overlooked.

The machines we were put into, meaning our human bodies, can only operate in a certain way, can only piece together our reality based on our current level of consciousness. So how real is this? Who knows how life on other galaxies might operate? Might it be less real? Some could operate at higher levels, others at lower, and these levels could create different worlds. Understand that you can only see 0.001% of existence. You don't have to see it to believe it, because that is impossible – our faculties aren't equipped for the truth. But something else within us is. Truth is in the space, the background for these faculties – our consciousness.

We know that there are millions of other galaxies. Our universe is *incomprehensibly* vast. When you think about our size in relation to it, life loses some of its reality. How can we possibly claim to know much of anything? And how can our small viewpoint be the ultimate reality? If one of your biggest problems comes from not being able to believe that consciousness is real, remember to let go of the word real. Everything is relative. The only way to know what is real is very paradoxical – you have to stop and let go of everything you previously thought of as real. Your limited body cannot see the light, and neither can your mind. Only the truth within you can see and listen to itself because the truth doesn't need anything else in order to exist, unlike our outer world which heavily relies upon our faculties.

Your birth here is temporary. This is a school. Depending on what you learn here, you may possibly go on to experience more advanced life celestially or you might be re-born here on the school of earth until you eventually learn its lessons. How fun and wonderful it is. But how frustrating it can be when we forget this. This is a temporary experience and nothing we see here is the truth of who we are. We must re-define real and make our minds vast and empty like before.

Be here and don't take any of it too seriously. This is only a beautiful play of form, or a temporary school, depending on how you wish to look at it. Life will throw lessons at you disguised as difficulties, and your response will determine if you are ready to move forward. Be here now. Be still and alert and silence your limited, doubtful self. Be humble so that you can evolve and learn as much as possible. Nothing is a mistake because everything teaches you something, and it has gotten you here, which is exactly where you're supposed to be. The toughest lessons are oftentimes the most valuable because you gain the greatest depth in the shortest amount of time. Remember that a fixed identity limits you and makes you one-dimensional and rigid. While you're here you can be anything and everything, completely unlimited, because you can be one with the truth. Of course you can do this because this is why you're here. To see the Earth as the ultimate reality in the grand scheme of things doesn't make much sense.

So if nothing is ever born and nothing ever dies, what is really happening here? When something dies, where does it go? Something within it, something which was holding its existence together, is gone, and only the shell remains. Then this shell breaks down until it too disappears. Nothing new can be created or destroyed, but conditions can come about which help to manifest that which was always there. You, as the observing consciousness, get to choose. All conditions are already here and we choose which ones we wish to broadcast into our reality. Everything is consciousness and is waiting to manifest itself. Until that time, it is in emptiness, and it is also here. Everything is here. The molecules that the match needs in order to create the fire are here. The here is the only place that contains everything, every condition, and each condition is waiting for the chance to manifest itself.

This also takes us into the labels of good and bad. Everything, every condition, is simply receiving a temporary manifestation. Labels create the tension that the harmony of the world relies upon. When a "bad" condition is manifested, it is through consciousness at the very lowest level. Our free will gives us the power to choose our conditions, but no matter what they are, they are still part of our consciousness. We have a choice, and when we are connected with higher consciousness, only those conditions which are beneficial to all will come through us into this world. And the wonderful thing is that when we cease to label conditions as being good or bad, each condition is beneficial in its own way.

So let's circle back to the beginning of this chapter. Why is it so important to let go of all conditions and stories? Because the truth is hidden behind these conditions and stories. The truth is the invisible and the condition is the temporary manifestation based upon our input. The truth is already here, abundantly surrounding us, but we're just not aware of it. All truth, all consciousness, is here, and we are part of it. We are not small, transient, manifested things. Our true identity is part of everything, part of the universal mind itself. All powerful, we are never victims. Far from it.

Nirvana is achieved when we become free of all notions, stories, and ideas because we have realized that none of them are "real", that only consciousness is real, and its essence is emptiness. This isn't about learning, or creating a better voice in the head to filter experiences through. Some people believe that the search is about thinking more positive thoughts. As Lao Tzu wrote in the Hua Hu Ching (translated by Brian Walker), "They will understand, at best, half the truth." Thinking positive means that there is still an identity within you which is trying to be good. It will trap you in the world of doing and labels.

Lao Tzu gave an example similar to a billionaire amassing a great fortune and then giving it all away. Wishing to do this is still clinging to an identity, one of a helpful giver to the world. Such a desire still harbors attachment to the small self and it is often the hardest to break because it *seems so good.*

156

But remember, you are a vessel. In every moment you either listen to a story, or you listen to your higher self, which lives in the ultimate level of consciousness which encompasses everything.

The nature of your higher self is love, compassion, joy, and peace. It is incredible bliss and it is nothing that you have to think about because it doesn't come through any concept or role in this world. Consciousness might still choose to manifest a billionaire through you into this world, and it might still choose to have you gift away your money, but all the while you'll harbor no attachment. Many enlightened people are outwardly successful, but the difference is that they don't take credit for this or assume it is their identity. You can be both a child, and a wise sage. You can be wealthy, and know the deepest spiritual truth. But you can only do this when you inhabit all points on the spectrum of life, instead of training yourself to fit a certain identity.

During the swearing-in ceremony of the Attorney General on CNN, Vice President Joe Biden kept repeating the same phrase as to why they had chosen her, "We believe her. She has shown us who she is and we believe her." He went on to say many wonderful qualities about this woman and her potential to lead us toward greater justice. But even an identity as wonderful as this is still temporary. Who knows what they'll believe about her at the end of her term. Could the truth be so very subjective? Maybe they'll believe she isn't so good anymore. But in the end, it is still just something they believe. It isn't the ultimate truth of who she is, but a present observation, a temporary manifestation, subject to a million fleeting conditions. If she too believes that this role is who she is, then when it is taken from her, she will suffer. We all confuse one another's identities, as well as our own, through our unconscious participation in roles.

Lesson 22: Watch all roles and identities from above with alert stillness and remember the impermanent nature of the world.

CHAPTER 23

Walking in Blindness

During the night when you become still, you nurture your higher nature and relax back into the source. This is why the stillness and relaxation of the night can be labeled as the feminine side of nature. Then, just as your body is ready to wake up and move, daytime and dynamic movement comes. This is the masculine energy of nature and it gives us the energy to create and participate in this world. How beautifully we flow through these two states, which seem to be perfectly made for us, and which are equally present in each of us.

We can say there is no empty space in the universe because everything is full of life, or pure energy. That would be true. We can also say that life is made mostly of empty space. That would also be true, seen from the point of view of the naked eye. Don't rely on words because they are deceptive. There is another way to know the truth: be the truth. What does that mean? Forget everything else. Die to everything else. Only the truth can remain in such a state because only the truth doesn't need our constant mental energy in order to exist. The truth is, and we are it.

So why do we fill ourselves up so much? If suffering is optional, why do we choose it? One part of the answer is due to conformity. The human race is one giant organism. We are connected at every level and as long as the majority remains unaware of the higher states within, we will all continue to suffer. When we believe there is no way out, then the way out cannot manifest itself in our world.

We cling to our old beliefs. But how often do these beliefs change? From one generation to the next we change our values drastically. What was frowned upon in one age, such as divorce or same sex-marriage, becomes accepted in the next, and what was believed to be impossible, such as flying, becomes a reality. People used to deny the idea of the Earth being in constant motion because they said that if it was, we would be able to feel the movement underneath our feet, or at least the wind going by.

Why do we cling so tightly to our misperceptions? Why can't we realize the truth immediately upon hearing it? Why do we feel we need to be a certain way? Look at most millionaires alive today and you will not see ease and happiness. In fact you'll probably see confusion and depression. Clearly, we have no idea what true success is, but we fight hard to think that we do. It is easy to change (meaning to move up in consciousness), but it is hard to be *open* to it in the first place – to recognize that there is a problem. Entire lifetimes are wasted like this, trying to force the beautiful world to fit into our extremely narrow and destructive points of reference.

Why not simplify, move consciousness upwards, be a vessel for solutions and possibilities? If we were doing things right, then over the years our lives would have gotten happier and easier. Instead we are surrounded by more false comforts and more neuroses. We have gone partly insane and we will continue to kill ourselves and our environment in our false search for progress. True progress would lead to happiness and bliss. How could we have settled for anything else for so long? With every generation we are taken further away from the truth and now is the time to begin our return swing home.

There are people who believe that we used to be much more advanced consciousness-wise than we are today, and that there were very advanced civilizations prior to our written history that had a connection to higher consciousness. They were able to use the pure energy of space and were very successful. Then there was a fall, the time in the cycle for cataclysmic destruction. It known as a cyclical process because there are many falls followed by remembrance of consciousness. They moved on, but there is evidence of their passage.

Very powerful and advanced things were happening on our planet. For example, in Ancient Egypt, it is puzzling to see how well developed the First Dynasty was. It's like they arrived here fully formed. In fact, by the Second and Third Dynasties, their art and civilization had begun to decline. If you look at the progress of a personal computer, then it's obvious that the first ones were very clunky and have progressively gotten better over time. But with Ancient Egypt, it's the exact opposite. They knew what they were doing from the outset and deteriorated over time. They had solution-consciousness to begin with, but somehow regressed to the lower states.

Some speculate that they somehow received perfect knowledge. No matter how they got it, they were extremely advanced. We only label them as being less advanced because they used pictures to communicate instead of written words. But words are very slow. Maybe there is a way to communicate without words, in which one communicates complex ideas at lightning speed. When Einstein was asked to describe the theory of relativity in a few words, he said it would take him at least three days to briefly describe the theory of relativity. It is incredibly hard for us to translate complex ideas into our common tongue, which we deem to be highly civilized.

When we switched to words, it is possible that our brains were rewired as well. Some even go so far as to say that our thinking became slower. We had to start explaining everything with words instead of instantly understanding. There are many more wondrous things about the Egyptians, such as their knowledge of Sacred Geometry. Their pyramids were not only perfectly proportional and linked to the star systems, but in many of them, the oldest stones were found at the top. How can that be? Shouldn't the oldest stones be at the bottom if they were built from the ground up? Unfortunately most Egyptian scholars ignore facts like this because they don't fit into their narrow frames. Any professors brave enough to study them risk discrediting their careers. We are limited in what we choose to believe and label as real and we actively persecute those who push our boundaries. We've simply forgotten how to live in conscious alignment with our energy source. We've made everything so small and dull, so outside of ourselves, when all we had to do was to go within.

There is evidence that 10-20,000 years ago there were very advanced societies that knew how to use this energy. Plato wrote about an ancient civilization called Atlantis. They were much more advanced than us, but they perished when the land sank and we haven't been able to find evidence of them. There are a few possible explanations for this. One of them is that we as a species go through planetary shifts. Every 13,000 years or so our consciousness shifts. We start at the highest states of complete bliss and we progressively decline, then rise again (which is hopefully where we are going now). In this way, we can return with an even more powerful consciousness that has been to the depths of the lows and has chosen to return to the high.

One hypothesis is that right after the proposed time of Atlantis, we went through such a shift and our consciousness significantly decreased and has led to the mass confusion that we experience now. We used to be much more evolved, but have fallen from grace and become separate. Imagine not having to rely on our slow brains and words to communicate. The lower age was the fall in consciousness which happened about 13,000 years ago. We had to begin using language and it would take us a very long time to get back to being even somewhat aware of higher consciousness, or our true power.

A civilization that is aware of higher consciousness functions differently at every possible level, because there are no problems or waste. Since we are so removed from it now, it is hard to imagine what life will be like when the majority of us awaken again. But Jesus Christ was here to awaken us when he said, "Wake up, sleeper, rise from the dead, and Christ will shine on you."[1] The Hindu epic, Mahabharata, states a similar truth, "there were no poor and no rich; there was no need to labor, because all that men required was obtained by the power of will; the chief virtue was the abandonment of all worldly desires... There was no hatred or vanity, or evil thought; no sorrow, no fear. All mankind could attain to supreme blessedness."

Presently, human life is highly unstable. We must either evolve, with the help of higher consciousness, or perish. Our current living is destructive and unnatural and every energy source we've found is limited and destructive on some level, which makes sense since we can only find that which corresponds to our current level of consciousness. We must stop relying on ourselves and the "sweat of our brow." There is infinite wealth and infinite energy, but it is not available to the finite mind. If we learn how to function with higher consciousness once again, we will find the solutions which we seek and forever turn our backs on lack and limitation.

If we are able to tap into this energy, we might travel to other galaxies, and their inhabitants could travel to us and guide us. Thousands of years ago, the Dogon tribe in Africa was able to accurately map the Sirius star system. Recently, when asked how they were able to do this so long ago without any help from modern equipment, they said that Sirius is where they came from and they believe that we are still receiving help from Sirius to this day. How the Dogon tribe was able to accurately depict this star system, as if they had been there and seen it, scientists do not know and they don't like the Dogon explanation. But it remains a fact. And scientists were only able to accurately map this Sirius star system themselves in the past couple of years with the help of modern technology, and it perfectly matches the cave paintings of the ancient Dogon tribes. Without the use of any modern technology, this tribe was able to discover this star system centuries before any of our scientists could.

This again seems to align with the theory that the Earth goes through cycles of cataclysmic destruction and rebirth. When Atlantis, which was a highly conscious civilization, disappeared during a consciousness shift, the planet embarked on a complete purging of technology, or things that aren't natural. Thus only the pyramids (since they were built from stone), as well as all plant and animal life, would remain – basically everything that was given to us naturally.

In the end it's all speculative and no one will ever really know what happened. The only reason to mention it here is to encourage you to keep an open mind. There's so much more to our history than what has been written about in books. Who knows if we're truly progressing? There is more evidence to point to the fact that we've been *regressing*, consciousness wise, and that now is the time for another consciousness shift, in which we'll return to the higher states from which we fell. It will be an end to our old world and a return to higher consciousness. We will remember that we descended into matter, our current shells, and we will remember the ancient philosophies, and see God as the "universal mind diffused through all things."

It is written in *The Kybalion,* which is a book of the Hermetic wisdom of ancient Egypt and Greece, "Do not make the mistake of supposing that the little world you see around you – the Earth, which is a mere grain of dust in the Universe – is the Universe itself. There are millions upon millions of such worlds, and greater. And there are millions of millions of such Universes in existence within the Infinite Mind of THE ALL. And even in our own little solar system there are regions and planes of life far higher than ours, and beings compared to which we earth-bound mortals are as the slimy life-forms that dwell on the ocean's bed when compared to Man. There are beings with powers and attributes higher than Man has ever dreamed of the gods' possessing. And yet these beings were once as you, and still lower – and you will be even as they, and still higher, in time, for such is the Destiny of Man as reported by the Illumined."

Just forget the truth you think you know. Of course we don't know the exact details of what happened here or what life was like 13,000 years ago. However, we need to stop assuming that we are more advanced now, and we certainly need to stop assuming that we're moving in a forward direction.

Lesson 23: Subscribe to Socrates, who said "I know that I know nothing." Today, let go and align with higher consciousness.

CHAPTER 24

Seeing the Grand Illusion

Fully accept whatever is in this moment for happiness. Happiness is the best way to improve the intellect, which is what we're after. This moment is absolutely unique, but a limited mind is never happy with it. This moment is the doorway to pleasant living. Don't let your life become a psychological nightmare played out in your mind, because you will suffer over something that doesn't actually exist. Whenever you resist this moment, you are taking yourself into your mind, which is subjective and oftentimes mistaken. Stop going there. Yield to the truth found in this moment.

Our highest potential is already within us. Just as the acorn contains the potential of the entire tree, our potential can only be realized when we merge with spirit. This choice will create the most magical and wonderful life possible, because it is what we are. It is our destiny, as long as we aren't afraid to let go of the false beliefs. No one would consciously choose struggle, so it is a mental exercise to realize exactly what we have been choosing to believe. We do have a choice, and having this realization is the first step toward truth. Now we know that we have a million beautiful choices and that our response to life is 100% our doing. You can take charge of your life and become a master here, and no matter what happens, you can live in unshakable peace.

When we live in any limitation, be it financial or relationship based, we are living in illusion. We have forgotten that we are made in the image and likeness of God, and so we have dedicated our lives to struggle and to victimhood. This is normal, because most of us spend all day covering up who we really are. We are here to evolve and to experience new and unlimited things every day. Every year and every moment is full of love, and this love is the force of life which is constantly expressing itself through us. But humans are so complex, we've actually figured out a way to repress this life force. We are the only species to have found a way to make life boring and stagnant. If we have figured out how to distort the truth to such an extent, just think of all the marvelous beauty and change we can create once we merge with the source of who we really are.

Look at natural life, offering the flowers and animals. They are guided by an energy that is vast, all knowing, and beautiful. But we are more complex than flowers and animals, and so far, this has hindered us. We have forgotten that we are the energy of love, and happiness, and life. We have been given the power to mold all of creation, and we have taken it and misused it to tie ourselves down because we feel we are not worthy. We are worthy, life intended this for us, and it's time to remember.

We are vast, all-knowing, and peaceful. Any other belief isn't true. We can't force this truth or think about it. We just need to allow it. Life is happiness, and we are able to create, enjoy, and become one with it. It is a miracle, a gift to be enjoyed. All of our desires, which are life's desires, will come to be if we allow happiness to be our dominant state. This isn't a luxury, this is a necessity. Life has been waiting for too long for us to love ourselves enough to accept this gift.

We are life and life is in everything. In every atom, it is the force that gives the instructions to be and to grow. This is our true identity. This one self that we are is within us but for some reason we have chosen unconsciously to believe something else. We believe we are bodies with an expiration date; limited victims with only a tiny portion of happiness if we struggle hard enough. If we develop our mental muscle and learn how to harness the power of the mind, we can connect with the higher self, or spirit. Once this connection is made it is like waking up from a dream. There is no more separation or conflict because we now have a purpose and everything we do reflects our inner joy, power, and peace.

The spoiled mentality of our current living leads to unhappiness. Where else could it lead? We are more detached and spiritually bankrupt than ever before. This has led us toward obesity and drug abuse, but eventually, this will also lead us to our awakening. Things might get worse before we reach a point where we will decide that we want to get better. This can only come about once we are tired of the struggle and the suffering. We will go from being spiritually bankrupt to being spiritual participants in this world. Plato wrote, "One of the penalties for refusing to participate in politics is that you end up being governed by your inferiors." We have been governed by inferior emotions and outer circumstances due to our lack of inner participation/diligence. Being spiritual doesn't mean that we sit on the sidelines – it means that we actively participate in the inner world and thereby make the outer world a better place.

So why haven't more of us awakened and pursued the spiritual path? It's because we have placed a lot of guilt on ourselves and even believe we don't deserve to be saved. Any mention of love sounds like mushy wishful thinking, and the result is that we reward ourselves for living lives of struggle. We believe that we must continue to work hard and remain unhappy. Most of us work our entire lives and have nothing to show for it. We live in houses we do not own, and in retirement we neither have the health nor the funds to live the life we would wish. What is the point of all this? Why should only a small percentage of people experience self-fulfillment?

When we become spiritually conscious, or present, it doesn't mean that we become lazy. We simply start to watch everything in life. The body, with all of its roles, doesn't seem to matter as much. Because no matter what problems it may solve, we have realized that these problems were created by the very mind which claimed to solve them. This means that we no longer go around in circles, creating problems and solving them over and over. We have connected with our true purpose and so spirit lives and fulfills through us. We will become tremendously efficient and our work load will be reduced. There will come a time when we will be shocked that it used to take 8 hours a day, 5 days a week, just to maintain our current standard of living.

To be present means to be open to hearing your purpose. You no longer give all of your energy and attention to the voice in your head that is constantly maintaining stories by holding on to the past and being fearful of the future and thus perpetuating the victim identity. It must work very hard to preserve itself from extinction and to prevent you from remembering the spirit that you really are, because as soon as you've had even a small glimpse of the limitless state, it knows it doesn't have long to survive. You will choose the truth because it feels so good, and this good feeling is precisely why it is the truth. You were made in goodness, as was the whole world. We are surrounded by love, which holds and creates all the life we see around us.

Once you know your purpose, your actions are full of happiness and ease because you are love and you harmonize and appreciate all of life. You no longer abuse yourself or any other lifeform in this world because you know the true identity of all things. It's the full realization of the biggest and most important purpose: awakening to presence. It's the fulfilling of your true purpose, not your false role, which brings happiness. Being able to distinguish between the two is key.

Remember, as Dogen said before, mountains do not lack the qualities of mountains. You are who you are. There is no effort involved and the end result is flawless as long as you don't interfere (which sounds a lot like "enter-fear"). Don't let fear take you over. Much like a butterfly trapped inside of a glass jar – in one respect she is working very hard, but in another respect, her hard work doesn't amount to anything because she is trapped. This glass encasement could be compared to fear and negative emotions, which trap us for the entirety of our lives and give us the false sense that our hard work is actually getting us somewhere.

Don't be swept up by negative emotions because they aren't true, and they need our temporary participation in order to continue their deception. There is nothing to be had in this world apart from spirit. If we remain separate, trapped, we will continue seeking more, seeking happiness. We cannot create or destroy anything. We can only be who we already are – and it is only the temporary story of the mind which tells us otherwise.

Our perceptions create our reality. Our perceptions are molded by our life experiences. This is why it is so hard for us to change and to accept new information. If we are steeped in illusion, we will hate those who enjoy high energy and solutions.

Remember that the voice in your head which forms your personality isn't real. Neither is the voice in the head which forms anyone else's personality (which is really the same voice and explains why so many of us live identical lives but believe ourselves to possess original thoughts). The reason why forgiveness and unconditional love are so important is that they are gateways to limitless living. Because the only way you could ever truly achieve them is by letting go of the false self and returning to spirit. This is the key to all happiness and success.

In school we aren't taught the most important thing of all: how to be happy inside of our own bodies. The Buddha and Jesus Christ were trying to teach us how to do this. Yet some fundamental Christians seem to regard Buddhism to be heretical devil worship. They misunderstand the deep truth that is within both messages. Although the words and methods are different, they are trying to get us to the same state: oneness with being.

If you want lasting peace, happiness, and power, you must rebuild yourself from the ground up. Strip away everything. It doesn't mean that you stop loving life or living it, but it does mean that you finally surrender and allow yourself to fulfill your divine mission. Your divine mission doesn't involve struggle, anger, or living in limitation. Leave yourself raw so you can rebuild your foundation.

As Thoreau said, the outer walls of our houses are often pretentious and we try to decorate the inside to hide the fact that we hold nothing of actual substance. The "house" is your identity, and when you don't know what it really is, you are forced to resort to fluff, to try and decorate it with illusions in order to make it more bearable. This is why Jesus said that our old dwellings, built on poor foundations, must go. Let the whole house be knocked down and then rebuild. As it is written in The Old Testament, "Except the Lord build the house, they labor in vain that build it." Your house is an analogy for your life. Of course you will continue to stay here and play different roles, only now your "house" or your identity, will be built on a solid foundation.

Yes, this means we're starting from zero because God will strip away our false identities. But would we really rather keep going in the wrong direction? Actually, the truth is that there is only one direction: straight. We are born here, time moves forward and we get older, and then we die and return to the very place from which we started. If we know that we are ultimately going back to where we started, wouldn't we like to know where that is? No matter what happens here we will be returning there. This is a temporary experience in form. Everyone has a different reason for manifesting on Earth as opposed to the millions of other options where consciousness could have gone.

Think about our current society. How many people are truly using the spiritual path and are actively trying to learn about who they are? And how many people have ever questioned the life around them? We are told that certainty is best, no matter how limited, and this closes the door to our mysterious nature. In A Course in Miracles one lesson states, "Spirit am I, Holy Son of God, free from all limits, safe, healed and whole. Free to forgive, and free to save the world." Just by saying this to yourself you save thousands of years of learning here on Earth. Because even if you do unconsciously choose to believe in illusion, either at the end of this life or in the next you will start seeking something more. You will realize that nothing you can ever achieve in this world can make you happy if you aren't aware of who you are.

In The Truman Show, Jim Carrey plays Truman, a man who doesn't realize that his entire life is all an act – that every step he has ever taken has been for the entertainment of an audience. As Christof, the man responsible for creating the show, says when someone asks him why Truman hasn't realized that it's all staged, "We accept the reality of the world with which we are presented." For the most part, people just accept what they are told and what they see in this world. Christof also says in response to an angry call about the unethical treatment of Truman's life, "He [Truman] could leave at any time. If his was more than just a vague ambition, if he was absolutely determined to discover the truth, there's no way we could prevent him. I think what distresses you, really, caller, is that ultimately Truman prefers his cell, as you call it."

The character of Christof is a pretty accurate representation of the ego, the entity which believes we enjoy our current entrapment and that our limitations are entertaining to us. It believes that it is making us happy. But at the end of the movie, Truman does make it out. He is only able to free himself once he stops being afraid to die, because living on the show becomes too scripted and unbearable. Truman represents our ultimate self, the part within us that craves the unlimited.

Most people will tell you we live in a crazy world and that they themselves would like to become better but they have no idea how. They feel hopeless and have lost their faith and so of course they see themselves as victims. There is no freedom for them, no healing or love of any kind. But as soon as we realize this isn't the truth, that there are many tools available to us for awakening, we can begin to return home. For the first time in modern history, spiritual knowledge is making its way into the mainstream. The truth, or paradise, isn't reserved for "heaven" when we die. We are actively pursuing this experience while we're still here – but this takes coming very close to death, stripping ourselves raw. A life spent in the seeming difficulty of this pursuit is better than hundreds of lives lived unconsciously. And now there is a new way – we no longer need to renounce our possessions, become a yogi, or a nun, or any of the other rigorous paths of the past. All we need is to become *aware* and *watchful* of ourselves in our present situation, so that we can make room for the ultimate self to emerge and guide us and clean up your affairs.

The self-imposed limits don't exist. We do not have to stay under America's laws, or any other country's laws. If we no longer agree with the office job, then we are under no law to follow it. Look within and discover your real laws. These false laws you have accepted to control yourself are selfishly using up too much of your precious energy. The more energy you give away, the more helpless you'll feel, and it will continue to go on and on in an endless cycle. The dark takes a lot of energy to maintain, whereas the light is effortless and actually brings more energy to you instead of depleting you. This is why children are so full of energy, because they don't give theirs away to laws that don't conform to their inner truth. They know they are perfect, whole, and complete. They know they live in a beautiful world with no limits. They feel their connection to the entire universe as they explore life in their bodies.

When you let go of the false laws and embrace the limitless, whole, and healed part of you that can forgive freely and love all things, then you will begin to make conscious decisions for the first time. And of course you will choose things that bring you closer to spirit. This is the opposite of what we currently choose to see in this world. We choose everything that will take us further away from spirit because we think we are unworthy and weak, and we are afraid to know the truth of who we really are because we think it will be bad. We are so mistaken, because the truth can never be anything but good. We are made in the likeness and the image of the Father. God is good, as are we, as is the entire world. When we choose to be unlimited, our illusions disappear. Without us, they have no place in which to exist. We are powerful and strong and wonderful. And all that is asked on our part is just to remember this and to use our free will to return to the truth and heaven on earth.

Stop letting illusions rule the world. Choose in favor of your well-being. Remember you're always choosing between love and illusion and you don't need to struggle in order to get a reward. Realize that you're constantly tempted to make up other laws and give them power over you, but at any moment you can live by completely different rules. Even when you argue with a loved one, you can forgive quickly. You can realize that a temporary conflict is situational, and you can value friendship above all else. Every stranger walking toward you can be seen as a friend. You can be free and wild and open to exploring this beautiful world.

You suffer only because of your belief in other laws. These other laws are ones you make up and impose on your world because you have closed off your true connection to spirit and now these false laws have tremendous power over you. Actually, "you" didn't make them up because they are impersonal. They are part of an energy field that dominates your mind without you even realizing. It not only takes over your thinking, but also your emotions. Soon, it controls the entire frequency functioning of your body. This is why so many people are walking around in constant pain or depression and are easily susceptible to anger. It isn't their fault because it isn't them. It's the false illusion walking around and controlling them, until they decide they've finally had enough and then they can choose to awaken.

Everything in the natural world follows its own natural law, and consciousness guides it and provides for it. But humans have decided not to listen to natural law. The first thing we must do is to figure out what our current laws are, and why we are choosing to follow them. Then, we can immediately do an inner cleanse and sweep away the false laws. The truth is like a houseguest that won't stay in a small, airless room. The truth is claustrophobic and it favors open space, which is why the Buddha remained silent. Even words of limitless freedom, wholeness, and love, are still only pointers and use up the space in your room. The truth is an experience, it is being, *it is.* Trust that when the false is stripped away and your house is clean and empty, then the truth will live in you. The only thing you must do is clean, clean, clean.

"God made man in His likeness and in His image." We were designed to live for hundreds of years. The ego takes a lot of energy to maintain and has decreased the human life span to less than 100 years. When we follow our true laws, we are happy and content. We know exactly who we are and why we are here and we are able to joyfully fulfill our function before we gladly return to the source. However, right now we live by false laws and when death comes we see it as a punishment. The very thing that created us is seen as a terrorist that threatens our existence.

Another major law we have forgotten and replaced is that death isn't real.

We were made in the image of the Father, and thus we are infinite spirits taking on various identities of earthly containers. Our only goal is to take on these identities while remembering who we really are, and then there will be nothing to sadden us once they are taken away. And these identities are fun, are they not? Who knows why spirit decided to place itself in the container of the form you see. All we know for sure is that it is a beautiful experience and the idea of death is what gives it such poignant meaning.

The laws of consciousness bring perfection and freedom because we realize that we are perfect and free already. When we start living in this way we are able to help heal the entire world. How do you know which laws you are following now? Look within. If you feel joyful and peaceful then you have been following the true laws of being. If you experience any anxiety or depression, then you have chosen to believe in other laws. Buddha said to pay close attention to your world, find out its laws, and then give your entire heart to it.

This is why you should never get mad at others – they've simply been reading from the wrong manual. They aren't aware of the real laws because they went to schools and were taught things by others who were equally asleep. The more we take ourselves out of our natural state, the more confused we become. No matter how comfortable life might appear on the outside, no matter how much "progress" we think we've made, we will not be happy. We will continue to unconsciously create more health problems and anxieties. What is the point in living like this? The daily maintenance and upkeep of our small containers comes at too great a price. It's almost laughable to see how seriously we treat this indefinitely short existence, while failing to recognize the timelessness within.

Remember that the voice in the head, our emotions, and our outside world, were created by faulty programming. This programing is so strong that it completely fools us into identifying with it and it eats up so much of our vital energy that escape seems almost impossible. When we try pointing this out to someone who is very asleep, or much identified with the outer forms of life, he or she will possibly attack. The false energy knows it isn't real and this is why it must work very hard to defend itself. Its temporary manifestation through us is the only existence it can ever hope to have; of course it will be on edge whenever consciousness, or the ultimate treasure within, is mentioned.

Connect with the truth through silence, surrender, and love. Choose to demolish your old house and build a clean new one with lots of windows. At first, the other system will try to deter you. You might feel uncomfortable, but by this point you realize not only that you want peace, but that you deserve it and that you are here to attain, meaning allow, it. There is nothing you must struggle for. All you need to do is to let go of your old house, your old identity, no matter how handsome or ugly it may be.

How much sense would it make for you to struggle, which means to create negative energy and further identify with the faulty programming? Do you imagine that somehow that energy will create something good and true? Of course it can't do that. People are identified with the faulty system which takes them further away from the truth. But this doesn't change the fact that spirit still lives within them, but in a deep part they cannot currently access. A tragedy might happen, which causes them to make some space within the faulty programing, and maybe for a brief second the truth can sneak in because part of the old identity has been demolished. Then this will start the return-swing back for them toward consciousness. Their actions will once again be in alignment with life. It is never too late. If you don't learn it here, you might need to come back in another lifetime so that you can finally remember it. But if you do learn here, then maybe you will spend your next lifetime elsewhere. Maybe there's a place in the universe where people are already living very consciously. To us, that type of place would truly be an astral paradise.

When we return to the source, it doesn't mean that we die. We simply merge our identity back with consciousness, instead of merely being a material form that participates in the world. This is what death is. Then comes birth, and we can come play and learn again. But while we're here, if we awaken consciously, then everything will be one with the truth of where we came from and where we are going.

To let go of the old manual means to let go of the personal laws which we have come to believe, and this can be hard. Remember that the old negative energy is very strong, and right now it controls both body and mind. But remember also that spirit is within. There is another path we can take to make life wonderful again.

Remember how subjective everything is, so let the spirit within you interpret it for you, instead of admitting the negative parasite. Become the master of your house, the king of your castle, and begin to censor who you allow in. What kind of king would you be if you gave audience to every measly thought that banged on your door and demanded your attention? While you are here in a body, it is true that you will need to interpret things to function in this world. But who will be your interpreter? Spirit or unconsciousness? The king or the pauper?

Think of it this way. The spiritual texts explain that your body is your house, and within this body is the house-manager. The house-manager can only be one of two people: God or the ego. They are equally available. However, if you do choose God, be prepared for a messy demolition and renovation.

When you return to the high frequency with which you were meant to live, you will only desire and listen to things that make you truly happy. How can you not? God is now the manager of your house, your body. In the same way that you wouldn't describe your house as being yourself, so too you will learn not to think of your body as yourself. From physics we know that everything is energy and vibration. Our current world reflects humans that are limited and as a direct consequence they are materially constrained. But being dense does not always have negative connotations. Sometimes it has positive, desirable connotations. As we vibrate with a higher frequency of love everything becomes light and joyful. This new energy creates a new life for us. It creates the life that we were always meant to live, and the world that we were always meant to enjoy, even when it is dense. We become certain, joyful, and unlimited, no matter what event comes our way.

We are just energy. We don't create anything; we simply manifest whatever we are able based on our current level of consciousness, and there are many lower and higher levels. If we wish to manifest other things, to broadcast other things in our physical world, then we begin to changing our energy. When we connect with spirit, our energy automatically vibrates at the highest frequencies of light and love. This is the most powerful thing in the world. This is why forgiveness and love are so important; they literally transform everything. In an instant we will know that we are already whole and complete, and all of the false striving will be gone.

Lesson 24: Today, let go of the heavy energy. You can connect with spirit and from now on manifest that which you were divinely designed to. This will feel very good and all limits will disappear. You will forgive the world because you will realize that there is actually nothing left to forgive. The madness was never real. The ego is no longer allowed admission.

CHAPTER 25

Greatness & Responsibility

At first, a shift in energy might be hard on the body. It's just like demolishing a house. You may find yourself experiencing symptoms as benign as the flue, or as life threatening as a car-crash. This is normal as your body adjusts to functioning at these higher frequencies. Just be gentle with yourself and remember that God is now in charge and He is building the perfect house, your perfect identity. Realize that you are making a vital change and you are finally fulfilling your function. This is no small thing and your entire body needs to adjust. Every cell will re-align itself so that you can fulfill your purpose. Your entire body will receive new messages and respond accordingly.

We now realize our immense potential and wish to help ourselves transform within this lifetime. This will include the need for self-love. You will be able to respond, and thus to foster response-ability. This means that whatever is happening in your life, you can choose your reaction – you are no longer functioning as a primitive machine. A computer cannot choose its function because it must follow the programming. When you no longer feel responsible (or response-able) this means you cannot respond to life and are unconsciously following a code, and in that sense you become dead. When you no longer respond to life, you forfeit your own power. The spiritual texts tell us that as adults, we have mastered losing our power, and this has caused an inner deadening of our vital energy.

Just as God is responsible for all of creation, we are responsible for what we choose to manifest. When we choose to awaken spiritually, a new energy will take over and things will happen willingly. This is heaven. We will be consciously aligned with everything happening around us. We will be free in our ability to respond instead of blindly acting out our emotions, and this will allow us to choose love and to create heaven on earth. This is our responsibility in every moment. This will bring salvation to us and to the world. Will we choose to embark on this very important mission? Or will we continue listening to the voice in the head, which is the very voice that we know to be trapped in false conditions and sure to create further unhappiness.

Unhappiness isn't noble. You are alive which means you can and must take responsibility. Filter what comes in through your senses before it creates your likes and dislikes. Stop holding on to old beliefs. Choose the beliefs in favor of life and see where they take you. Let go of unhappiness. That is your only mission here. How amazing would it be if we all accepted this and were able to manifest our highest, most loving intentions? We are better able to help if we are happy ourselves. Any other state contaminates the world.

At first, it might not feel good to say, *I am responsible for this*. Your life might not be the way that you want it, and so it might be easier to continue to feel helpless, as if some outer force is responsible and you are the victim. But if you can bravely take this first step, it will take you to the opposite end of the spectrum. You'll swing from victim to powerful agent. You will say, *I am responsible! I am able to respond. I create my world and by being in touch with my intentions and desires I can manifest that which I was meant to. I will create only that which makes me happy and is in line with my purpose – which is ultimately the same as the purpose of the universe.*

There is no right or wrong way to live your life. If you feel love and joy within, then you are connected to spirit. Whatever you choose to do will be in alignment with universal purpose because you will feel it in every cell of your body. You will be light and alive. You will be fully responsible for everything in your life and this will bring back your tremendous power. Was it previously tremendous? Yes! What it ever not tremendous? No! You are a Son of God and this power will flow into everything you do because you will be a celestial being once more, temporarily inhabiting this speck of dust, and enjoying it. You will be in conscious alignment with the universe and you will help to bring about God's will, which is heaven on earth. All suffering, which is really just a form of continuing education, will be gone. You will flow like a child once more, and you will be as wise as the best among us now are; abundant, spiritual, and wealthy in every respect. The main purpose will be happiness and you will no longer unconsciously create anything else. The illusions will be gone and you will find your peace.

In this state, you are free to forgive the world. You no longer have the need to hold on to grievances because you realize that they were never real. They were subjective, existing in the mind and belonging to the small self, and like puffs of air, they will disappear forever once you stop giving them the ability to exist. You will be in this moment and you will realize that you no longer need the past or the future. You are connected with consciousness right here, in the now, which is the only place that is real to you anymore. All previous identities will be gone and you will feel light and carefree. Now you'll be able to accept and yield to life and it will be joyful. The struggle of the small self will be gone once you stop deriving your sense of identity from it.

You will marvel and rejoice at not having to live in that way anymore. You will realize what a blessing it is to awaken and you will want to share this gift with the world. You will enjoy the world and the world will enjoy you. You will be a bearer of peace and freedom and good things and wholesome situations will gravitate toward you. People will want to be around you because they will unconsciously feel your high vibrational frequency and wish to be in tune with it. You will help people solve their problems because you will teach them that their problems are self-imposed. You will show them the truth. If the people are ready to hear the truth, then they will be free.

You are free to forgive the world because you know that by forgiving you let go of your own limits and victimhood. You realize how wonderful consciousness is. You realize that nothing you could ever create in your mind can come close to its power and love. You will no longer need to grasp with your limited mind. The right programming will finally be in place, and it will allow you to yield to the truth and let it shine through you. You will know that any anger, force, or aggression is false. There is only peace and all is well. God is the *doer*. He is the author of your action and the creator of your world. He is the mother, father, child, rock-climber, lawyer, waitress, and whatever other roles you see. Perform all action, good and bad, with perfect detachment (meaning to observe your thinking). Be present. The body is God's temple whether you realize it or not.

During times of hardship, people often turn away from God. When they do this they are moving further away from the truth. Instead of using the situation to crack the shell of ego, they move further away in the other direction, toward more illusion.

Remember instead that any challenging situation can be used to stop your swing, or your momentum toward unconsciousness. This whole time you've been struggling and moving away from the truth. Use the suffering as a way to stop the momentum of illusion, and start the return swing toward home. Learn about the power of love from your children. Connect to consciousness before your physical body here dies. Use every challenging situation as your perfect spiritual practice. It is perfect because it is what you have been given to help you to awaken. Then a healing energy will surround you, and the right people and messages will begin to enter your energy field so that you can heal and be open to the truth.

Any action you take when connected with being will be powerful. Any action that comes from reaction, meaning from an unconscious identification with the ego, will not be coming from the real you but from the perceived importance of the outer situation. Unfortunately, this false importance and misperception is in control of the majority of our population. They are constantly reacting to situations around them, from their work, to their families, to their own compulsions. They feel that these outer things are somehow happening to them, and they proceed accordingly.

The transformation begins when you decide that you no longer wish to react and to give away your power. You realize that any situation is subject to perceptions. You decide to get firm with your mind and not let it run wild anymore. Everything will pass and there is no use in holding on so rigidly. You are spirit now and you have more than enough power to deal with any situation. But mostly, you realize that no situation needs to be dealt with. It just needs to be experienced, and the right energy (action) will flow into it. This is power. This is not human, it is super-natural. You know that no matter what this human is doing or saying or experiencing, you are at home elsewhere. Sometimes your voice may need to be firm, but you will still be connected to the deep peace within, so there will be moral support there. Your inner judge will be flushed out. You will do as Rumi said and, "Raise your words, not your voice." You won't lose yourself in any emotion. This pleasantness will elevate you to the perfect state of intelligence – before it was hacked with faultiness. You realize that this world cannot alter your true self and it is only here for you to become more aware of it.

Lesson 25: My true self cannot be altered. It will remain perfect and eternal, and I can let go of all fear. I don't need illusion because God is now in charge of my life.

CHAPTER 26

The Holy Fire

If you look within long enough, you'll realize that the Christ, or spirit within you, wishes to be happy. It doesn't struggle. So how did we lose it? We created other conditions, ones that would surely take us away from happiness and further blind us to our purpose. Anytime we feel sad, we are choosing illusion. Perception doesn't concern the physical. It deals with what is behind the physical and what brings us to this seeming materiality in the first place. We must intend to connect with this metaphysical, higher nature within us and banish everything else by become selective over our perceptions. This part is crucial because everyone must awaken in order for the world to be at peace.

We are not these heavy, small people that we see walking around. There is another dimension to all of us that we've simply forgotten. We must let that mysterious dimension, the space within us, be our identity. In that simple, naked awareness, we will remember God.

We create everything in our lives. If we believe in illusion, our lives will mirror struggle and sadness. If we align with spirit, then the happiness that we are will flow into everything that we do. Wherever we go we will bring light and joy with us. This isn't something only given to a few people. If Jesus thought this gift was only meant for him, then why would he have gone through the trouble of sharing it with the world? Jesus felt connected to spirit and he lived all of his days miraculously. If he didn't think this was intended for everyone then he probably would have gone off and lived a peaceful life somewhere. But he stayed because he wanted us to live like this too. He saw clearly how unnecessary our beliefs about suffering and separation were. He stayed because he knew that the inner state he was experiencing was intended for everyone. He wasn't preaching so that a few of his words would go down in the great books. Time and again he said that this was not coming from him, but from the Father, meaning that he had banished his ego. He was detached and God was the doer. He didn't want us to read and to recite, he wanted us to transform and live as he did, so that we could honor the Earth and our beautiful experience here.

The movie *Wild (directed in 2014 by Jean-Marc Vallee)*, which was based on the book and life of Cheryl Strayed, depicts a woman who had lost her mother and was going through a divorce. She decided to embark on the Pacific Crest Trail with no purpose other than to be in the wild. During her time outdoors she was able to clear her mind and in the end she said, "How wild it was, to let it be." Her story is so powerful because it is mainly about overcoming obstacles and developing the qualities necessary for personal transformation. This is how evolution works for us all – through conscious struggle. This is also why the Buddhists say that the lotus needs the dirt out of which it grows.

For Cheryl, the small personal parts didn't matter anymore. This is the only way that you can let go of a painful past. You know that any situation is not part of your true identity. And look at what a beautiful and inspiring lesson came out of all of her life situations. We can never judge anything by whether it appears to be good or bad. Suppose that she had been able to live a 'normal and happy' life. She wouldn't have had the profoundly deep transformation that she did. The most wonderful thing is that at the end of the movie, her past hadn't disappeared, nor did it need to. She realized that there was something deeper. The identity that the world gave her was not who she really was. This isn't something that is easily put into words. Being in the wild helped her to find her courage and freedom, her own hidden powers.

She eventually realized that life only gave her what she needed to experience in order to grow, or to expand her consciousness. The poet Coleman Barks puts it this way, "Love grows from the ruins of personality." Cheryl says this in another way, "God is not a granter of wishes. God is a ruthless bitch." Life gives us exactly what we need in order to grow and to learn. The pain in our lives is meant to be a tool for our evolution – a way for us to die to our old selves. Without the pain, few of us would have the motivation necessary to take on a change in consciousness. Just like the fish in the sea, something forced a few of them to try to live on land; something about the sea had become too inhospitable. This is evolution, and if you allow it, your pain will transform your consciousness and you will help the human race to evolve to new heights.

Use your suffering, your current inhospitable situations, to build depth, and then let them go. In the movie Wild they showed a quote of a poem by Emily Dickenson, "If your Nerve deny you, go above your Nerve." This shows the separation between you as an observer, and your nerve, meaning your emotional tendencies. There is a place above that you can go, watch, and hover, because it is above all of the drama. Emily Dickenson's poem ends with, "If your Soul seesaw, Lift the Flesh door. The [coward] wants Oxygen, Nothing more." We are all trying to heal, and healing happens when we expose our hidden, unconscious tendencies to the light. The cure is to let it out, let it go, let that dark coward hiding within see the light of day.

Clearing the mind is so simple – it is subconsciously the solution that everyone seeks. This is why suffering is necessary, because without such a state of affairs, we would not see the opening for something new because our minds would not be clear or silent enough. And actually, most people in their suffering fail to grasp this tremendous opportunity for awakening. But our suffering could potentially be the starting point for our higher selves to emerge above that which we have produced thus far.

Acceptance fosters our necessary evolution. When we finally understand that we are responsible for our situation and that going forward we can change things, then we can finally begin to use our untapped powers. We awaken to our hidden treasure. This is all evolution is.

You don't need to be tied down and deadened by all of the illusory, conflict-ridden, nonsense of your inner world. It takes a very brave person to step back because most of us are stuck listening to this inner madness on autopilot. But you can choose to heal and accept happiness. Let go of useless ideas because no matter what, at some point you'll have to. When you are on your deathbed, with the return-home ticket in your lap, you'll realize that you could have dropped those other things long ago.

Our lives need our conflict in order to create the drama and suspense which we find so entertaining. For now, the majority of people evolve only very little. They believe that people don't change, and if you start out insane, unfortunately you are destined to remain like this. It's amazing how much energy we spend trying to make the impermanent into something permanent. If the impermanent was important, and if we really couldn't change or do anything about our stories, then God would have been kind enough to not give us the desire to try.

Of course we can change. While we're here life wants to live through us and change us in every moment. The good news is that you don't have to wait until you are on your deathbed to have this metaphysical experience and connect with your divine nature. This is no longer an experience that is reserved for Yogis and Buddhas. If the Earth is to survive with humans on it, we must all try to do this now. We can die to the illusion and live the remainder of our lives as spirits who are temporarily here on a vacation of sorts. Then, we can laugh and reminisce on what life was like when we thought of the Earth as our permanent residence. And Earth is so thrillingly beautiful that it is impossible to put into words. We just have to be here and watch.

Many of the most wonderful people both living and dead have gone through the most tremendous unhappiness. Unhappiness leads you to a place where you can finally listen and understand, because unhappiness is unconscious resistance to life. You think something should be one way, but it isn't. You think that the Earth would be a better place if it could just listen to you and to your ego. But as soon as you accept your unhappiness and stop resisting the life that is behind it, you will be able to make it through. And not only that, but you will be powerful and peaceful because you have journeyed far and have come back to the right place.

There are many different kinds of suffering, both mental and physical. In mental suffering we are stuck holding on to painful memories or are anxious over the future. In physical suffering, there is something painful happening to the physical body. For most of us, the suffering is mental. For some, it is physical. In both cases, acceptance is the only way to transcend suffering. Jesus not only accepted his physical suffering on the cross, but he said, "Forgive them Father for they know not what they do." He knew the truth, and he didn't let illusion get in the way. He completely let go. Suffering can be our best spiritual practice because it is the quickest and most powerful one.

We are entitled to miracles and we can allow them to replace all grievances. If you do not think you are worthy, if you still think some sort of punishment must be endured, realize that this is just another aspect of unconsciousness. This is the unconscious part of you punishing yourself and the world. Do not try to fight it because it will only take you further away from the truth. Today, choose to stop fighting anything. Simply remember that consciousness abides in a state of happiness and the best way to get there is to be responsible and to intend that state. Be thankful for everything in your life that isn't happiness because this will be your direct spiritual practice and it will help you to build depth, evolve, and to bring about a new consciousness. Examine it and see if you can let it go. Be like an alchemist and transform the suffering into happiness. You have traveled to the depth of unconsciousness and back and your light will burn brightly and guide the way for the whole world.

Lesson 26: I am involved with life and I let life happen through me. I am open and responsible and alive. Under God, I create everything through my choice for peace. I am thankful for the journey I have taken to get me here. I am guided with ease and clarity. There is nothing to hide and all has been forgiven.

CHAPTER 27

The Paradise of Delight

"And Death is not real, even in the Relative sense – it is but Birth to a new Life – and You shall go on, and on, and on, to higher and still higher planes of life, for aeons upon aeons of time."

-The Kybalion

Become involved with life and let life happen through you. Religion has tried to teach us to be open and to surrender our perceived limitations. What would be the purpose of religion if it remained something that we didn't know how to use? The lessons are meant to be applied to better ourselves and the world. These are the best self-help manuals out there, yet even the most devoted followers often fall short of actually using their transformative powers and changing their state of consciousness.

Life is constantly expressing itself through us. We age through the years and with time we evolve into something new. Life should be connected with our desires because these desires, whether conscious or not, determine everything. Are we aware of what our desires are? Desires come from two places: The ego or the spirit. The desires of the ego will never bring lasting happiness, because if they did, that would be the end of the ego. The crazy mind has worked very hard over the years to keep us enslaved and it doesn't want to enable our liberation. As St. Augustine said, "Lift up your sick self, just as you are, and let your desire reach out to touch the good, gracious God, just as He is, for to touch Him is eternal health."

Be careful what you wish for because it will set the sails for your entire life journey. It will either be toward ego pursuits, or toward spirit. Don't wait until the end only to find out that you have been off track. If we're not becoming happier, more enlightened, then we're just going around in circles.

We have no idea who we are or why we were placed here. Deep down we feel that we don't deserve this gift so we cover it up with the workings of our minds. But remember that you were made in the image and the likeness of the Father. Take this seriously! God is love and you have His power within you. Don't shy away from this responsibility. And the good news is that the abundance of spiritual teachings now eases your way. It's so much simpler than before because now you don't have to do it blindly and in isolation. There have been many who have gone before you and share your work.

Remember that your outer world will reflect your inner desires. Most of your desires are unconscious, clouded, and complex. What is the point of dedicating your life to them? Desire love and peace and it will be yours. We have innate desire within us, which spirit helps us to fuel. Every cell of your body knows what it wants – it wants life! Our bodies are the most complex organisms that we know of, and every cell is programmed to stay alive, and this desire to live parallels life itself which seeks to grow and to enjoy. It doesn't wish to over-expand, which then becomes cancerous. And it doesn't wish to become stagnant. It wishes to remain in perfect balance.

Our fears hold us back from our true desires, the ones we were programmed by life to achieve. Just like the seed of a tree, our full potential is already within us from day one. When we fulfill this potential we manifest our inner purpose. When we don't, we remain unhappy and confused, no matter what is happening in the outer world. Sometimes people give themselves "safe" desires, because they see themselves as small and separate. They don't realize that they are part of life and that the whole universe is here to help them. The universe needs the tree; it doesn't need the seed to remain dead in the ground. These safe desires of ours leave us miserable because we know that we are more than this.

The ego has its home in the body and it makes you believe that this is who you are. It has distorted things to such an extent that this separate idea has become your entire identity. The body is temporary and someday it will leave the Earth. The spirit is formless life and it is eternal; this is who you really are at your core. The real you (spirit) and the body (temporary crazy mind) are two different things. For example, a small child upon learning her name might say something like, *Suzy* wants milk. She doesn't say *I* want milk because she hasn't fully identified with this body as being who she is. She retains her connection to the source, for a while at least, because she recognizes that Suzy the body is not the same as Suzy the *I am*. This will go on until we teach her our process of identifying with the body and help her join us in our version of the world. But our true "I" doesn't want or need anything here because it is far beyond the limitations of the manifested world. We have forgotten so much of our true identities that even at death, we cry over losing these limited roles.

Thoughts and emotions are of the body and are fleeting. Look at them this way: since they are not permanent and are highly subjective, they are not real. So why do we believe in them so much to the point of giving up our most wonderful real identities? We place labels of right and wrong, good and bad, instead of openly embracing all of life. We allow wrong-headed notions within us to guide and interpret everything. This is what happened when Adam and Eve ate from the tree of knowledge of good and evil: a misguided notion within them started labeling all of life. They were no longer open and receptive and they began to be ruled by the mind, which is very good at labeling and creating identities. They lost their connection to the source and went the other way; they decided to make their thoughts and emotions the ultimate truth and they were allowed to so this because of their free will.

Our false and temporary identities have become the only things that are real to us, for now. But we have all the time in the world. Our universe has been around for billions of years, and although we might temporarily be unconscious, we will return to full consciousness and then journey even further still with the depths that our fall has placed before us.

When you live from the mind, you are giving away all of your power. Everything becomes reactive because you are completely identified with form. Real action is power because it comes from you. Real action can come only when you are responsible and not reactive to the environment around you. It comes when you realize the part you play and who you really are. However, as of yet, most people are reactive and have placed their power outside of them. In one moment, such a person might be completely in love and in awe, and in the next they are in pain or frustration over some happening which has challenged their beliefs. What happened? Some outer event didn't go according to what their mind labeled as good. This caused intense suffering because the mind and its labels are placed on such a high pedestal that we blindly follow wherever they lead us.

Of course things will be different from how your very limited mind can predict and expect. Don't you think that by this point life knows what it is doing? The best thing to do is to let go and trust in the divine flow of life and to surrender your sense of self to God. Tell yourself that you don't know, and it will be the most liberating experience. You will let go of the ego and you will let spirit be in charge again. Remember that every moment you are choosing one or the other. Our quiet awareness is the only thing that can bring us closer to God. It blinds us to the cares of the world and helps us to finally receive our joyful gift. We must keep ourselves rooted in this contemplative silence, so far from the world, so that we don't accidently loose our awareness again and fall back into illusion. Sometimes the mind will trick us into thinking, but no matter how wonderful this thinking might seem, try to stay as centered as possible in the quietness of your being. Master all illusion by refusing to feed it so that you can be whole and know God.

Hard episodes are a gift from consciousness because they are a doorway to letting go. They can temporarily crack your small identity. As long as you identify with difficulty and believe in suffering, this door remains closed because you have placed your belief in the outer, transitory world. When you are ready, the door will open, and these hard episodes will be transformed into completely different experiences. Nothing can be created or destroyed; it can only be transformed back into the light. And yes, there is a way to live free of any suffering. Only a few people on Earth are living in this state, and they assure us that it is intended for everyone. The question is whether or not you wish to reach it in this lifetime.

Lesson 27: Today, you choose spirit. This means that you are on a path to live beyond limitations and labels. And most importantly, you teach and show others that this is possible.

CHAPTER 28

A New Life

When you are caught up in a human reaction such as anger, it takes you over. Everything becomes tight. There's no space; no presence. If you can notice yourself getting angry (or any other heavy emotional feeling) then try to pause and watch what it does to your inner state. First, it might create pain somewhere or a tightening in your chest. Next, if you aren't cautious, it will permeate your mind and take over your thinking. Suddenly, everything will become horrible. Instead of being angry with yourself for being in such a state (which is really only more unconsciousness) welcome it, because being is right above this. If you can go above this emotion and thinking and watch the negativity, knowing that none of it is who you really are, being fully aware that consciousness wants perfect love and happiness for you, then this will be the greatest gift and will greatly assist you in your living-practice. It is wonderful to read spiritual texts and to meditate, but you must begin to apply these lessons in your life so that they can begin to transform it. You don't become peaceful by reading and meditating, but by choosing to remain peaceful in the midst of chaos. Choose being and allow yourself to be lifted to a higher realm while remaining here.

If you choose anger or anything that isn't love and happiness, then you are choosing to remain in the human realm because it is the only place where such things exist. You can act and live just like a regular human, or you can be super-human, a perfect being enjoying a brief human experience, realizing that none of this is who you really are, accepting this world as a state that you must pass through on your way to perfection, and simply enjoying the journey. Then, the new human race will emerge and prosper.

Remember that when you experience a negative emotion, don't use force. Watch it from above. If you succumb to it that's acceptable, so long as you were able to watch it for even a few seconds. This will help you to build greater awareness. Start being compassionate and interested in the world, instead of the thoughts in your head. Be present and see what is really happening inside of you. Leave the life of desperation behind and stop restricting yourself. Be as free, peaceful, and powerful, as you were intended to be.

Fear, loss, suffering, and death are all optional. This is what you must remember. There is either God, or there is illusion. You can only know this by connecting with your higher self, which knows the truth and has never believed in or been hurt by the world. There is a way to live in this world without any suffering. The other identity, the plain human part, needs to stop being so loud. Quiet it down so that you can hear the true voice and return to happiness.

You must provide a way for *being* to enter your body. That is all you have to do. It's especially nice because there is nothing you have to think about or to understand. This experience is beyond words because it is beyond our current, and very limited, human thinking. Compared to the vastness of the universe, the human mind is smaller than a speck of dust. There is no way that we can logically deduce the truth to fit the mind.

How will you know if you are making progress and connecting with being? The entire world will become friendly. The fear which held you back for so long will be gone and you will become spontaneous because you are free to enjoy your divine self. Wonderful things will come through you and other people will be drawn to you. This elevated state of consciousness is the next level which we must reach as the entire human race if we are to survive.

Our foolish way of living has been going on for thousands of years. We saw it at the time of Jesus as well as now. But in cosmic time this period was no more than the blink of an eye. It is a slight glitch in our functioning which we hope to heal in this present age, and then to go on to live in peaks never before imagined. We will stop giving up the very best parts of ourselves, the parts that are happy and complete and contain all of the answers. We will cease creating problems for ourselves by valuing the wrong things. We will accept happiness, and we will stop being machines, slaves to our own minds. Einstein recognized our mechanical nature when he wrote, "In human freedom in the philosophical sense I am definitely a disbeliever. Everybody acts not only under external compulsion but also in accord with inner necessity."

We don't realize that we haven't made many conscious choices. We think that we are free, when in fact we are the slaves of faulty mental systems. Who would consciously choose unhappiness? Another very enlightened statement made by Thoreau in Walden was, "One may almost doubt if the wisest man has learned anything of absolute value by living."

We must unlearn. We must stop living heavy and wasteful lives of illusion. We must stop being afraid and conforming to the current state of the world. Yes, it is the current manifestation, but it is not the truth. We will be guided by a new voice toward the abandonment of our old ways. We have always been compelled to live, but now we will do so with the greatest ease and happiness.

Like the lilies in the field that Jesus spoke of, you are effortless. As Thoreau also said, plants bear fruit in air and light, far from the ground. Our wisdom cannot grow on the ground, it needs space, it needs to reach the bliss that is beyond human thought. Leave the Earth and it's heavy ground and go toward heaven, which is spacious and vast – it is a state of *no-mind*. Choose to relax because nothing is asked of you that you do not already have. Everything that was ever created already *is*, and its potential is within you. The universe created you for a purpose and you already have everything within you to accomplish this.

You can only know the truth when you observe your mind. You can be your own spiritual teacher when you learn mental discipline. Self-realization should be the ultimate goal of all spiritual striving. This means that you have control over your own self and freedom from your own karma, which is composed of negative energy and false action. Liberation is the ability to no longer be run by your own compulsions; it is complete freedom, peace, and control over yourself.

When you don't have control, you cannot see false action and emotion as false. They become real to you and are all consuming. We were bitten by a poisonous snake when we ate from the tree of knowledge of good and evil and were separated from God. The venom is still within us, it is our karma, and the antidote is awareness of the one true self, or cosmic consciousness. Everything in this world speaks a language and this language comes from God. It is alive and it lives through us all. But for some reason humans have chosen to create their own language based on limitation and suffering, and it filters our entire existence. It has become so habitual to not see love that we've forgotten about the option. The good news is that we can return to the state of perfect bliss because now that we are free to choose, why would we want anything else?

The truth has been within us all along, but we have simply forgotten. The Buddha, upon achieving enlightenment, said that we are already perfect Buddhas, but we have forgotten due to the craziness of the mind. This is why we must embark on the mysterious journey through the wilderness, for although it may seem daunting, the end will be the greatest happiness which we could ever hope to experience.

We are here in this lifetime to decide who we want to lead our form: the higher nature, or the little self. We are approaching a time when more and more of us will choose to remember the heavenly aspect of ourselves. Whether this happens as a result of improved human self-realization in an environment of material sufficiency, or against a backdrop of desperation due to material insufficiency, is up to us. The only evolution left for us is that of our inner state. This realization cannot be made if we remain asleep – all it requires is the desire for awakening.

Lesson 28: Today I realize that I can only love the world by letting it go.

CHAPTER 29

Experiencing the True Self

"Let him who seeks continue seeking until he finds. When he finds, he will become troubled. When he becomes troubled, he will be astonished, and he will rule over the All."

The Nag Hammadi Library, Gospel of Thomas

Your spiritual search can begin once you stop being completely attached to the world. It may be a long journey and you ought to be well prepared. Who knows how many lifetimes you've spent searching for or running away from God. In the Bhagavad Gita, God urges the higher self to fight, to not become a coward, and to remain calm in both victory and defeat.

This is God speaking to the higher self within the person who is not sure he can fight this inner battle because even his worldly compulsions are treasured. But he must! He must choose righteousness, calmness, and peace. He must not remain forever trapped in endless cycles of suffering, and learn nothing by living. He must go on to higher planes of existence.

But still, you may wonder how you can give up the pleasures of a world you can see for one that you can't; but which you are told will surpass worldly pleasures 1000 times over. In the Bhagavad Gita, Arjuna (the highest self) isn't ready to let go of worldly pleasures, yet Krishna (divine inner wisdom or God) tells him that these pleasures are his enemy and will destroy him; meaning that the ego is here to destroy us, although it tries to make us believe that it is bringing us pleasure.

In the Gospel of Thomas, Jesus said, "If you bring forth what is within you, what you bring forth will save you. If you do not bring forth what is within you, what you do not bring forth will destroy you." With the complexity of a Zen koan, he invited us to see the truth within, and to let go of the false.

Remember the pendulum swings from the very beginning of this book: the more you can resist the swings between illusions of good and bad, and remain even-minded and calm, the closer you will come to self-mastery. Alexander Pushkin, the Great Russian author, once said that there is no happiness, except for peace and freedom. He wrote "The Poet", which translated from the original Russian by Andrey Kneller (with the last three lines taken from a translation by Yevgeny Bonver) goes:

> *Until the poet's summoned thus*
> *By great Apollo to be martyred,*
> *Within the world of bustling fuss*
> *He stays immersed and faint-hearted;*
> *His lyre's silent, hushed and cold,*
> *His soul lies deep in wintry slumber,*
> *Among the humble of the world*
> *For now, he is, perhaps, most humble.*
>
>
> *But let the Word divinely drop*
> *And on his harking ears fall lightly,*
> *The poet's soul will rouse timely,*
> *As though an eagle, woken up.*
> *He's bored amid the world's diversion,*
> *He longs for simple speech instead,*
> *And to the feet of idols worshiped*
> *He never bows his proud head.*
> *Instead he runs, untamed and grave,*
> *Full of confusion, full of noise –*
> *To the deserted waters' shores,*
> *To woods, widespread and humming loud...*

We are all poets. Apollo, the Greek god of light, healing, and beauty, wishes to speak to all of us but we are too busy in our world of bustling fuss. Our souls wait in slumber until the Word, or consciousness, finally reaches us. Then we rise, simple and brave, no longer worshiping the idols of the world. Jesus said that we are each of us like him, and that if we look within, the mysteries of life will be revealed to us as well. All true teachers have told us in one way or another that we are able and destined to achieve the truth. Untamed, full of confusion, unable to explain the unexplainable, we must simply run toward the truth as best we can.

God can only be known in peace and bliss and such states come when we stop identifying with the noisy circumstances of our lives. Our minds must become as calm and deep as an ocean, and as widespread and endless as space. It is from a calm center that all right action emerges. We can reflect an appropriate response to every circumstance. We don't need to give exactly the same glance or reaction twice. We don't need to mold ourselves into the typical human existence. We can return to our prefect, unknowable simplicity.

Our actions are the movie, they are God's cosmic entertainment, and we must turn them over to him. This is what is meant by detachment. In this way, we can move through the world with, "desireless desire" and there will be no ego or self-seeking in anything that we do. We will watch it from the consciousness that we are, and God will act, create, and move through us. God is in everything in the manifested world and we must be able to see Him in everything if we are to see Him at all.

The very fact that you are attracted to and are reading this book means that you have come very far already in your spiritual search. You are ready to watch with detached awareness and attain infinite bliss. You are ready to free yourself from your attachments and desires.

Watch the world joyfully, and it will joyfully mirror your identity. In this way you become one with the life around you because the essence of life is love and happiness. If you seek this you cannot fail to find it because it is the truth. Currently, the world is primarily run by people who are unconsciously asleep. Until this is changed, even in the midst of tremendous wealth, people will remain unhappy. There will be some without homes, some without medical help, and some that will starve. This will continue to happen on our planet every day until enough of us awaken and realize that the meaning of life is happiness and compassion for all, and that we must awaken together. Until this is fixed nothing else can possibly be called progress.

We have romanticized notions and like to think that the greatest and most enlightened people have come to Earth fully formed, when in truth they didn't. The majority had very depressing lives, and their desperation is what brought them to God. Don't let anything in your past hold you back – use it to push you forward. Remember that suffering can be your treasure and your key to awakening. Become humble and don't let the world lure you in; awaken to the untamed and endless present moment.

In truth we haven't come very far since the days of working with plows for a living, only the nature of our work has changed. The Puritan work ethic is still around and it shows up in how much we praise and admire those who work 12-hour days. Are they achieving anything of a lasting good for the whole within all this fuss? Probably not. Are they happy? They've gotten everything they were told would give them the prize. What now? And on it goes. In the Gospel of Thomas, Jesus also said, "Do not tell lies, and do not do what you hate, for everything is known before heaven." There is nothing wrong with working, so long as it is done consciously and to fulfill your purpose, instead of blinding you and making you restless so that you cannot possibly hear the voice of sanity and peace.

On the other end of this spectrum there are those that are too passive and have fallen below the level of thinking and into laziness. This isn't the right path either because they aren't consciously awake. Although these examples seem like opposites, they are actually very similar. Both the overly active and the overly passive are run by the mind. They are not connected to life; otherwise they wouldn't be trapped at the two ends of the spectrum, which are deficiency and excess. The spectrum is one. Let go of the labels and you'll find yourself aware of everything.

Don't allow roles to place guilt on you. When you are free and pure, in the stark and unfamiliar aliveness of your being, you will be free from the roles and imaginings of the mind. This inner work is the highest work that you can do here on Earth. If you have become weary and disillusioned with the world, this is helpful, because as Pushkin wrote: you're bored of usual diversion and long for simple speech instead. Everyone understands this deep down and knows that they are called to return to God, but only a few are able to surrender illusion and follow this call because they are not able to surrender the rational mind. The experience of God is nothing that you will ever be able to speak about. This isn't to suggest that your associates will be uninterested, they will, and as will you. You will yearn to be able to describe the indescribable, but in order to do this, you must first let go of the rational mind, which is your tool for brining things into finite comprehension. Just accept that this is too extraordinary for description.

We can move along the spectrum, or the pendulum, without ever having to label it and become stuck. When we resist changes of energy within us we create stressful circumstances. Within us is the perfect code to fulfill our life's mission. We have the energy and intellect to achieve this, and although we might not remember, every cell of our body does remember and it constantly strives to remind us. We must watch ourselves move along the spectrum in different roles – but we cannot accept them as being our true identities.

How do we achieve balance? We stop believing that we have to choose. Affirm to yourself a new belief system: *I can fulfill my purpose and be happy because there is nothing in the outside world that can cause me any suffering.* Remember that the fulfillment of your purpose is the only thing that will bring you happiness. No struggle or stress is necessary; in fact, it is a deterrent to happiness. This is obvious but in the rationality of our crazy minds we can easily confuse or forget it.

We can raise a family and achieve our outer purpose. This is what is so fun and beautiful about life. We are meant to have many roles. Life loves to experience itself through us in many ways, and it's only fair for us to let it do so. Life is why we're here. It is beautiful and complex and it is just like us. If we were meant to embody a single identity, then we wouldn't be equipped with this incredible potential for multiplicity within us.

There will be moments to act and moments to be still. Moments to use the mind to create something, and moments to not think about anything. You will hear the Word of God, although you will be unable to explain it, and it will guide you in everything. You must be comfortable with not knowing, with sweet sounds and confusion. Everything around you is made up of consciousness and the way it manifests in the outer world comes though different moments, not through words or thinking. If what you have manifested thus far in your life isn't what you want, then you need to let go. But don't overthink it. You are meant to remain open so that the different energies of consciousness can pass through you and create through you. This is how the whole universe came into being, and as Lao Tzu said, from the One came 10,000 things – from the singularity arose all multiplicity.

There is a small group of people who have already attained the highest potential of human development. But this small group is growing, and out of this group will emerge a new human race, consisting of people possessing pure consciousness and freedom. The time has finally come for more people to awaken and to join this group.

Most of us have chosen another identity, or rather, and unbeknownst to us, this unconscious identity has chosen us. We can return to peace by surrendering. In the grand scheme of things we cannot hope to understand all of life. We cannot understand it with our minds; and yet we wish to grasp it, and it is this desperation which holds us back from the truth. The truth is a gift that we must yield to. Let the universe fill your mind with abundance. If you pay attention, there is nothing that can be denied. If everything in the universe happens on purpose, is it possible that you're somehow living apart from this rationality? You have God potential within you and if it remains unrealized it will create suffering until you remember to connect with it. Suffering is here to connect you to the truth. As soon as you see this, you cannot suffer. Use it and transform your life. Be kind and focused. Learn skills and plan your life but be here and be free to change course in an instant – welcome the wild and untamable within you. Let life emerge through you, both chaotic and highly structured. Embody both ends of every spectrum and let go of all limitations and notions of what life is supposed to be.

As Dogen wrote, when the moon is reflected in water, it is still just one moon, not two. Your realization of this, that you are just the water, the canvas for the reflection of life, is your return to God, to the pure life within you. You leave your own separate world and you return to God. The inner stillness where you live is God, and the outer world where you walk is God. Jesus, along with Buddha, Krishna, and many others, taught us that to know God is the only real reason to be here. This is our path to happiness; our liberation.

Toward the end of the Bhagavad Gita, the highest self stands and says that his illusion have been demolished. God has restored perfect perception, and all doubts are gone. He is now ready to act according to what God desires.

You are perfect; all you need to do is to remember. The past has brought you here and it has taught you valuable lessons. Now, begin living in the mysterious, unknown, present moment. May you be free of all imprisonment and limitation.

Lesson 29: Today I surrender everything. I am a willing participant of life. Divine order is with me and it guides me in my growth, realization, and return.

ACKNOWLEDGEMENTS

I would like to thank Timothy Maloney – without you this book would not be possible for many reasons. Thank you also to Mom, Josh, and Willow. Most importantly, thank you to all of the wonderful teachers who have gone before me.

NOTES

Chapter 3

1   Luke 22:44 (New International Version). Holy Bible, New International Version®, NIV® Copyright ©1973, 1978, 1984, 2011 by Biblica, Inc.® Used by permission. All rights reserved worldwide.

Chapter 6

1   Mark 8:34 (New International Version). Holy Bible, New International Version®, NIV® Copyright ©1973, 1978, 1984, 2011 by Biblica, Inc.® Used by permission. All rights reserved worldwide.

Chapter 9

1   Luke 17:20-21 (New International Version). Holy Bible, New International Version®, NIV® Copyright ©1973, 1978, 1984, 2011 by Biblica, Inc.® Used by permission. All rights reserved worldwide.

Chapter 11

1   Proverbs 3:6 (New International Version).

Chapter 13

1   Matthew 6:19-21 (New International Version). Holy Bible, New International Version®, NIV® Copyright ©1973, 1978, 1984, 2011 by Biblica, Inc.® Used by permission. All rights reserved worldwide.

Chapter 15

1   John 14:12 (New International Version). Holy Bible, New International Version®, NIV® Copyright ©1973, 1978, 1984, 2011 by Biblica, Inc.® Used by permission. All rights reserved worldwide.

Chapter 16

1   John 5:30 (New International Version). Holy Bible, New International Version®, NIV® Copyright ©1973, 1978, 1984, 2011 by Biblica, Inc.® Used by permission. All rights reserved worldwide.

Chapter 23

1   Ephesians 5:14 (New International Version). Holy Bible, New International Version®, NIV® Copyright ©1973, 1978, 1984, 2011 by Biblica, Inc.® Used by permission. All rights reserved worldwide.